RARE BIRDS

*Dare to Break from the Flock
and Find Your Purpose*

MEGHAN WALSH

Copyright © 2025 by Meghan Walsh

All rights reserved. No portion of this book may be reproduced in any form without written permission from the author. Reviewers may quote brief passages in reviews.

Disclaimer and FTC Notice

No part of this publication may be reproduced or transmitted in any form or by any means, mechanical, or electronic, including photocopying or recording, or by any information storage and retrieval system, or transmitted by email without permission in writing from the author.

While all attempts have been made to verify the information provided in this publication, neither the author nor the publisher assumes any responsibility for errors, omissions, or contrary interpretations of the subject matter herein.

This book is for entertainment purposes only. The views expressed are those of the author alone, should not be taken as expert instructions or commands. The reader is responsible for his or her own actions. The author shall not be liable for any loss of profit or any other commercial damages, including but not limited to special, incidental, consequential, personal, or other damages.

Adherence to all applicable laws and regulations including international, federal, state, provincial, and local governing professional licensing, business practices, advertising, and all other aspects of doing business in the U.S., Canada or any other jurisdiction is the sole responsibility of the purchaser or reader.

Neither the author nor the publisher assumes any responsibility or liability whatsoever on behalf of the purchaser or reader of these materials.

Any perceived slight of any individual or organization is purely unintentional.

*To my mother, Mutard who always supported my dreams
no matter where it led me in life.
Thank you for always being there for me.
Love you always.*

Contents

Your Free Gift 1

What is Purpose? 2

    You Are Good Enough 24

    How to Utilize This Book 29

    Exercise: Setting Your Intentions 31

Your Why 33

    Difference Between Your Why and Purpose 36

    Leadership and Your Why 46

    Exercise: Finding Your Why 49

Leveraging Your Strengths 51

    Character Strengths 53

    Your Unique Strength 61

    Exercise: Leveraging Your Strengths 71

Silver Lining to Your Weaknesses 73

    The Silver Lining Model (ACE) 83

    Exercise: The Silver Lining to Your Weaknesses 87

Leaning on Values and Principles 89

    Principles to Guide Your Direction 94

    Exercise: Values and Principles 104

The Ikigai Model 105

Understanding the Patterns 117
Exercise: Filling Out the Ikigai Model 119

Purpose Through Hurdles 121
Transforming Into Rare Birds 125
Teaching Through Hardship 133
The Dawn 135
Exercise: Learning From Hardships 139

No Regrets 140
Your Legacy 150
Exercise: Writing Your Obituary 154

Clarity in Purpose 156
Using Your Intuition to Connect with Purpose 163
Heart Connection 165
Exercise: Clarity on Your Purpose 169

The Stories We Tell 170
Fear of Failure 179
Exercise: Uncovering the Resistance 184

Creating a Spark Through a Vision 186
Vibration Resonance 190
Exercise: Building Your Vision 205

Your North Star 207
Intentional Action 212
Sacred "Yes" 217
Consistency 219
The AIDE Framework 221
Exercise: Intentional Action 229

The Next Step 231
References 232
Thank You 236
About the Author 237
Client Recommendations 239

Your Free Gift

As a heartfelt thank you for purchasing this book, I'd love to gift you the *Find Your Purpose Workbook* along with *guided meditations* to help you get the most out of this experience.

I want you to be successful on your journey. For me, learning is all about putting wisdom into action. This interactive PDF will support you as you work through the exercises at the end of each chapter. This book is about self-discovery, and the real work begins when we start to look inwards.

To get exclusive access to these bonus materials, head over to: www.fearlesslotus.com/freegift

Chapter 1

What is Purpose?

Finding your purpose is a profound and transformative journey. It goes beyond identifying a career or activity you enjoy. It encompasses your deeper motivations, values, and the impact you wish to have on the world. It is a guiding principle, giving meaning in your life and the actions you take. It's essentially what lights you up.

Not everyone finds their purpose early in life or at a certain time. We are all at different stages of finding purpose. It can also adapt and change as you grow. It can be difficult to create meaning and purpose in our life when most of us have been taught to focus on money. Follow the money. Get a good job. Have a stable career so when you retire, then you can finally live your dreams.

Most of us wait or prolong where we truly want to go in life. There is a fear we will not get there. We won't be successful or find something better. We limit ourselves because a lot of us might not even know our purpose.

Some of you may be in a job that is not fulfilling for you. Each day may feel like an endless chore or feel meaningless. There may be a nagging feeling like you are meant to do something different. You are meant to be on a different path, but you are not sure what it could be. That was me for most of my life.

I did a lot of things from a career perspective based on what other people told me I should do. They told me to go to school and so I did. They told me to get a university degree and so I did. They told me that in order to be successful I should focus on business. And so I did. I went on to get my MBA because that is how you get a better job that makes more money. I thought I would be guaranteed a job with an MBA.

I am a logical person, so I took the most logical routes in my life. I told myself this was the best way forward. I would get all this financial wealth and then I would be happy. I told myself for many years when I have this job, when I am making this much money, then I will be happy. When I have the corporate executive job, then the doors to happiness would open. Yet "when" never came.

I told myself that these were all smart choices. Choices based on logic. Yet my job never fulfilled me like I had hoped. After coming out with debt from my MBA, I couldn't even get a corporate job. I was working as a cook in a wing bar in Calgary. I made the bold move to leave Canada and go live in London. A lot of my friends from my MBA program had moved there. My roommate from university said I could stay with her until I got my feet under me.

I landed a job in television, and at first, I was over the moon. It seemed like a dream job and while it was fun, in the end it wasn't fulfilling. I based my happiness on the role I had, the money I made, comparing myself to everyone while feeling a deep sense of emptiness. I told myself I needed to work harder and play harder. The workaholic, alcoholic lifestyle. While I had an amazing adventure, I still felt this sense that I was missing something in my life. I didn't know what it was, but I knew in my heart I was meant for something else.

I didn't have the tools at the time to go deeper within myself to find it. I was taught to look outside for happiness. The infamous saying, "I'll be happy when." I kept chasing it, yet nothing ever filled the insatiable emptiness. I worked in many industries, and you would think I would find my purpose or happiness within one of them. While I was good at my job and exceeded expectations, no amount of money, promotions, or roles fulfilled my purpose.

It took me many years to realize my purpose was to help others. To walk with them on their path and teach what I have learned through my own challenges. Stumbling in the dark and faceplants into my mistakes led me to what truly lights me up.

The hardest part is to look inward. Quieting the chatter of the outside world and look inside. To be aware of what is coming up and face the shadows head-on. My spiritual journey has unfolded in many beautiful ways. Yet it can feel like tumbling down a hill at light speed, bracing for impact. I know it sounds terrifying and perhaps it is, but I wouldn't trade it for anything. I have never felt more alive, more authentic, and like I'm truly stepping into my power.

This is the impact of living your purpose. Terrifying and exhilarating at the same time. Especially when you know there is a hidden path for you. Your journey may not be the same as mine, but it is a conscious choice to start going down a new path. Whatever that may look for you and whatever you believe in.

This book will teach you tools and frameworks to help you understand your purpose. You will learn to release the stories holding you back. Start building a vision once you understand your purpose and how to create intentional action toward it.

Your purpose is a guiding force shaping our mindset, our outlook on life, and how we see the world around us. When we are more fulfilled, we tend to have more happiness in our life. We create more joy because we are taking the time to do the things important to us. They create meaning in our daily activities and what we prioritize to cultivate the joy around us.

Once we know our purpose we can weave it into our daily life. We can find a new career or role giving us meaning based on what truly matters most to us. We get to decide how we want to embody purpose in our everyday life. We get to choose if we want to incorporate purpose into our activities, our career, or a new business venture.

Most people are not born with this sense of purpose. If this is you, that's okay. It wasn't me either. It took me forty years to figure out my purpose and my why. I finally understood what lit me up and how I wanted to implement it in my everyday life.

The fact that you are here now is all that matters. It is never too late to be on this journey of self-discovery. Most people don't even get this far, so celebrate where you are now. Celebrate that you are deciding to take that leap into the unknown and discover new things about yourself. To start crafting a new life in a different direction. It takes guts to do this. It takes perseverance and belief in yourself.

We are creatures of habit. When we create change our reaction can be to rein it back in. It can start to feel uncomfortable, so we want to step back into the shelter. Yet this does not create the learning opportunities to continue forward. To reap the rewards and live the path we were always meant to find.

Purpose instills meaning in our activities, our actions, and our time. If you are looking for a meaningful career, start with your purpose. You may have looked for new opportunities. You may even have found them, but the satisfaction wasn't there. It can feel like a need that hasn't been met. An emptiness unable to be filled. We are searching for something more interesting, challenging, and meaningful. Perhaps you are searching for a company aligning more with your own values. Wanting to create value within your work.

This is the fulfillment we are all seeking on a daily basis. It is wild how many people are unhappy with their jobs. Yet they tend to stay in similar roles instead of finding something more aligned with their purpose. We grew up with this notion of following our dreams but along the way we settled. We told ourselves it was good enough.

Purpose can be daunting to find because it feels abstract or too grand. It can feel overwhelming to think each of us has such a deep purpose within us. This might be a reason why not a lot of people go after their purpose in the first place. They feel it is too substantial for them to obtain. This is a fallacy because your purpose does not have to be grand. It can be as big or as small as you want it to be. It is what gives meaning to you. It is what lights you up. Whatever that might be.

We will be going through different elements to help you gain clarity on your purpose. What shifts you will take to incorporate your purpose and how to take action. From a career change, stepping into retirement, or incorporating purpose in your spare time, this book will be your guide. There are multiple pathways to your purpose.

My purpose will be different from yours, and that is okay. What matters is after you find your purpose, what do you plan on doing with it? When we have the courage to not only take the steps to find our purpose but also live it, this is where the magic happens.

One of the reasons why people tend not to pursue their purpose is because of money. They think their purpose will not make the same amount of money as their current situation. We tend to follow the wealth first because we think it will make us happy. Money will never buy you happiness. While it may make things easier in certain ways, it is not the solution to life.

When money becomes our main driver, it creates a rat race. Constantly chasing money to ultimately find happiness. Instead, we go around the marigold ride. We are told it will make us happy, but money rarely does. It doesn't give us the sustenance we are truly seeking.

A study found a sense of purpose as an indicator had an increase in income[1]. Since purpose tends to give us more meaning, it has a positive correlation with our financial outcome. Kahneman and Deaton's 2010 study found after $75,000 annually our happiness plateaus[2]. Theorizing once

---

[1] Hill et al., "The Value of a Purposeful Life: Sense of Purpose Predicts Greater Income and Net Worth," *Journal of Research in Personality* 65 (2016): 38-42, https://doi.org/10.1016/j.jrp.2016.07.003.

[2] Daniel Kahneman and Angus Deaton, "High Income Improves Evaluation of Life but Not Emotional Well-being," *PNAS*, Princeton University (2010): 3-5, https://www.princeton.edu/~deaton/downloads/deaton_kahneman_high_income_improves_evaluation_August2010.pdf.

our needs are met, more money doesn't increase our happiness. You want to feel secure in your finances, but it doesn't give you that fulfillment. Living your purpose gives you higher satisfaction and engagement.

Most people want to be happy, but they don't know how to achieve it. They chase the money, the power, the prestige, but they don't look deeper to see what they really want. They don't ask the question, "Why do you want it?" Most people would say, because they want to be happy. Yet the truth is most people don't know what makes them happy.

We tend to follow what we are told will make us happy. I did this for years. I told people when I was in school my goal was to be an executive. My friends would say, "An executive of what?" I had no real answer: "An executive of whatever." That was a flag. Alarm bells should've been going off saying, "Maybe go deeper?" Yet I didn't have the tools to go deeper. To look inside and stop listening to everyone around me telling me what I should do. This was not in my cards at this point.

I volunteered for many years at a local homeless shelter called Yonge Street Mission. They had a scholarship program for those attending university while struggling with poverty. If they maintained a certain grade average, they were given a scholarship and a mentor for the year. I volunteered to be a mentor to this young woman named Jennifer majoring in Business Technology.

I really enjoyed meeting up with her on a weekly basis as she was navigating her first year of university. It was a unique experience as the world was also navigating the pandemic. She was a very pragmatic and logical person. She would ask me insightful questions. One question Jennifer asked, "What is the one thing you wish you could tell your younger self from all of your experiences?"

I said, "The one thing I wish I would tell my younger self is listen to your inner guidance. Your mind will give you the logical answer, but your heart will always point you in the right direction. Follow your heart to where you truly want to go in this world. Don't blindly follow the advice of others because they are not living your life. You are." I wish someone had told me that. It can be scary to follow your true purpose and what will make you happy, but it's worth it in the end.

If you plan to do a certain degree or program, stop to ask yourself, "Why am I choosing it? What is the deeper reason for my choice?" If the answer is *because I can get a high-paying job*, or *someone told me it was a good choice*, neither of these should be the reason. Go deeper within yourself to find the answers. You may find a good job with a good salary, pension, benefits, etc. But if you absolutely hate it, the toll is not worth it in the long run. We only get to live this one life. Find what truly lights you up in the long run and follow it.

While I wish I had this advice, I believe we are all meant to follow our own path. Even with all the mistakes and challenges because that is how we learn. I don't feel regret because it took me longer to find my purpose in life. At least I found it and now I am taking steps to follow it.

Some people will go through their entire life hating their career because it is unfulfilling. I am grateful I took the path less travelled and found my own way in the darkness. It helped me understand a valuable lesson of questioning my mind. Allowing myself to peel back the layers to see the bigger picture instead of my own nagging thoughts.

I did have a lot of fun in my career and loads of experience in a variety of industries living in different countries. It was fun and fancy-free, but it wasn't fulfilling. Every time I got a new job, I would tell myself now I can be happy. Yet there was always something missing. There was this feeling like I was meant to be on another path, but I didn't know what. Looking back, I could see hints if I'd been paying attention.

This book is your hint and you've made it here. You are reading this book because you know you were meant for something more. Your path is meant to have meaning in your career and your life. It can lead you to success in a completely new direction. Helping you see a hidden path.

I want you to first set your intention for this book as you read it. Write down in a journal or on a piece of paper that you can see every day, "My intention for this book is to find my purpose." Intentions are very powerful, and they help us to focus our energy in the right direction.

Setting your intention at the beginning will help you to create momentum. You will start to have more inspirational thoughts as you go along. You may meet people aligning with where you want to go. You may not have clarity at this point, but that is okay because you are going to get there.

You have taken the first step. We are going on an adventure together. This is going to be your guidebook to craft your purpose and use that as a foundation. It is going to inspire you, drive you, and give you the passion that will create so much abundance in your life. It is an amazing feeling when we first put that intention out there. The intention tells the universe that you are ready to start in a new direction. This new path will give you deeper meaning in what you've been searching for. You are going to start to become more attuned with the world around you and enrich your life with meaning.

I hope you enjoy the ride and the exercises at the end of each chapter. Try to complete each one before you continue to read. They are building blocks that will be the foundation for your success. The exercises will help you dive deeper within yourself. Understanding all the different elements playing a role in your purpose.

You are taking the leap of faith of knowing that you were meant for something more. A lot of people wish they could do something that fulfills them. I found the more I spoke to people about their jobs, the more it became clear that many were unhappy with their current position. Either their role had lost meaning, they felt underappreciated, or it no longer sustained them. If this is you, this book is for you. I am going to help you gain clarity into the different aspects of what can truly become a new direction. One that is fulfilling, creates happiness, and brings meaning into your life.

Purpose gives our life meaning, passion and drive. When we are fulfilled within our work and our daily activities, we will never work another day in our life. We won't be counting down to retirement because we are happy doing what we love. We are motivated and inspired every day. We appreciate not only ourselves for having the courage to find our own purpose but also for living it.

It is okay if you are not sure what your purpose is right now. The fact that you are reading this book is the first step of the journey. It will give you a roadmap to find what lights you up. What gives you meaning and how you can apply that to your career or daily activities.

The challenge for a lot of people is when they see their career as a sunk cost. They have already spent too much time in a role, a division, or an industry. They start to inch closer toward retirement feeling they cannot break free because of the years they invested in a career. So instead of pivoting, they count down the years they have left until retirement.

I have friends and family who stay in their careers even if they loath it. Why? Because they have already invested in that career trajectory. Freedom for them is retirement even if it is ten to fifteen years away. Personally, ten or even five years to freedom is too many for me. Not to be morbid but we don't know how long we have left on this Earth. It could be one breath away or years away. Let's make each moment count.

When we stay in a role that is toxic, not meaningful, or taxing, it creates a lot of stress and unhappiness in our life. We spend on average close to 2,000 hours working in a given year. That is a lot of time and energy spent on something unfulfilling. Lack of engagement can also lead to higher stress levels and burnout. As you can imagine, work-related stress can also put strains on our health and overall well-being.

Specialization is another aspect that can be challenging to navigate. It is great to have a lot of experience, but it can pigeonhole our growth. Employers only see one skill set you are good at and breaking free can be a hurdle. Later in the chapters we will look at a powerful model. It will help you uncover transferable skills to open new opportunities that give you meaning. Our life experience can transfer into something more satisfying for us to pursue.

We only need to dig a little deeper within ourselves to find it. One of the main things I want you to keep in mind is that you are not alone. You have people to support you on this journey. They can give you additional feedback as you work through the exercises.

We may have blind spots when we start to peel back the layers. Connecting with friends, family, colleagues, and mentors we trust can give us valuable insights. We may not even see how truly amazing we are in certain areas until we have someone else point them out. We can have these aha moments when we get a second opinion. Imposter syndrome can also sneak in, deflating our confidence without us even realizing it. We may see ourselves in a certain way and others might have a different perspective.

Engaging from different perspectives can help you gain additional insights. Allowing you to go deeper in understanding about yourself. The more you are willing to put in the work into this process, the more you are going to get out of it. You can even have an accountability partner to help you stay on track. You can ask them beforehand if they would be open to meeting with you as you go through the book. Let them know you are pursuing your purpose, and you value their insights.

Purpose is important because it gives us meaning in life. Spending time contributing to something fulfilling and worthwhile that drives us. When we create space for this purpose to be weaved in our life, we have a higher sense of gratification. We are fulfilling a greater way of being.

Unfortunately, most of us were not taught to find our purpose at a young age. We were taught to follow the money as a main driver in our life. A lot of us ended up falling into positions and then staying there because of the golden handcuffs. This can be through the corporate pension, paid vacation, salary, or stock options. We get stuck feeling like we don't have any other options of finding something more fulfilling, so we stick it out. We don't have clarity around what is meaningful to us or what jobs could light us up.

Social media has taught us to look farther outside ourselves. Comparing our lives with those we admire, those we work with, friends, and family. We see what they have and feel like we are lacking. This is why we try to fill our lives with things we think we want. We want a bigger house, a boat, a high-paid job, etc. We want more stuff because we think that is what will make us happy.

I have fallen down this rabbit hole, only to have the exact opposite happen. I didn't understand why until I realized all I was doing was putting off my own happiness. I was doing everything for things instead of for me. I was living a life I thought would make me happy because it was financially secure. I was doing something I didn't love because of the golden handcuffs I put on myself.

We compare ourselves financially to other people chasing money in pursuit of happiness instead of being happy. We tend to seek happiness outside of ourselves through external factors such as money, a bigger house, a flashier car. Sadly, this becomes a moving goal post. The secret is happiness comes from within.

We have a narrow vision of how money comes into our life, yet there are a multitude of ways of finding financial abundance. So, most of us stay unfulfilled and create stories in our minds, keeping us stuck where we are. When we can love ourselves unconditionally. Accepting ourselves for exactly who we are. By going deeper within our own psyche, we can transcend through the meaning we cultivate.

One of the best parts of living your purpose is how it amplifies all aspects of your life. It creates better relationships because you are more present. Your meaning not only affects you but the people around you. This creates a positive effect on the people in your life.

When you have purpose in your personal and work life you are more likely to be engaged, productive, and happier[3]. When you are fulfilled and establish meaning in life, you cultivate more joy. Stats Canada reported 84 percent of people who acknowledged high life satisfaction also had a strong sense of meaning and purpose[4]. The correlation between happiness and purpose allows us to gain meaning in our life. It becomes an amplifier creating positive benefits because we have enriched experiences. We are more in the

---

[3] Humberto Charles-Leija et al., "Meaningful Work, Happiness at Work, and Turnover Intentions," *International Journal of Environmental Research and Public Health* 20 no. 4 (2023):17-20, https://pmc.ncbi.nlm.nih.gov/articles/PMC9963286.

[4] "How happy are Canadians?" Statistics Canada, last modified March 20, 2024, 2:00 p.m. (EDT), https://www.statcan.gc.ca/o1/en/plus/5891-how-happy-are-canadians.

present moment instead of the mind within our day-to-day life.

One of my favourite things to witness is the spark in a person's eye when you help them shift their perspective. They start to see their own greatness within. Breaking down the limiting beliefs so they can truly shine. It is almost as if I can see the light turn on inside them. I can feel the joy it creates with them. It is a beautiful part of my purpose I get to see on a regular basis. These moments create so much meaning in my life. It is a great feeling to find your purpose and have the courage to live it.

Purpose also has an impact on our overall health. A sense of purpose in our life is associated with lower risks of dementia[5]. The Health and Retirement Study found participants with the highest levels of purpose experienced significant health benefits. They had a 46 percent reduced risk of mortality and a 23 percent lower risk of stroke. There was also a 17 percent reduced risk of lung disease and a 28 percent lower risk of physical functioning limitations. Additionally, they showed a 16 percent reduced risk of cognitive impairment and fewer chronic conditions overall[6].

---

[5] Sutin AR et al., "Sense of Purpose in Life is Associated with Lower Risk of Incident Dementia," *Journal of Alzheimer's Disease* 83 (2021): 249–258, https://pmc.ncbi.nlm.nih.gov/articles/PMC8887819.

[6] Eric Kim S. et al., "Sense of Purpose in Life and Subsequent Physical, Behavioral, and Psychosocial Health: An Outcome-Wide Approach," *American*

When we connect with our purpose daily it can help us to be happier. Creating a positive impact through the gratitude it also brings. I personally feel more grateful on the days I relate back to my why and purpose. According to a meta-analysis published in the *Journal of Clinical Psychology*, people with a strong sense of purpose experienced notable health benefits. A clear understanding of purpose was linked to better mental and physical health. It also correlated with lower levels of stress and higher overall well-being[7].

Gratitude is a powerful practice linked to an increase in overall well-being and happiness[8]. When we derive meaning from our purpose, it naturally allows you to be grateful for what you have in your life. It creates a spiral-up effect, amplifying these positive emotions.

Our minds have a negative slant in our perspective. Research found we need three positive thoughts to every

---

Journal of Health Promotion 36 no. 1 (2021): 137–147, https://pmc.ncbi.nlm.nih.gov/articles/PMC8669210.

[7] Ian D. Boreham and Nicola S. Schutte, "The Relationship Between Purpose in Life and Depression and Anxiety," *Journal of Clinical Psychology* 79 no. 12 (2023): 2736-2767, https://onlinelibrary.wiley.com/doi/full/10.1002/jclp.23576.

[8] Harvard Health Publishing, "Giving Thanks Can Make You Happier," *Harvard Medical School*, August 14, 2021, https://www.health.havard.edu/healthbeat/giving-thanks-can-make-you-happier.

negative thought in order to flourish[9]. Meaning we need more positive thoughts to thrive. These negative thoughts were originally programmed to keep us safe and survive. Yet now in our current place in time it can inhibit our growth. When we are aware of this it can help us to purposefully shift this negative slant in our thinking.

How many times has one small thing set off a chain reaction for a terrible day to ensue? Perhaps you spill your coffee and stain your shirt before going to work. Now you are late because you can't find your keys and are frazzled. You think to yourself, "It's going to be one of those days." Instantly your mind is in a negative space and may stay there for the rest of the day. You mentally have written off the day as terrible. You start to look for things to go wrong to justify how you feel in that moment.

It has happened to all of us, and we are all human. How we choose to move forward with this knowledge is our choice to make. When you have a strong sense of purpose to follow throughout the day, it can bring you back to centre, helping to build your resilience dealing with challenges.

You see things from a higher perspective, allowing you to shrug off small inconveniences. The ones that could have

---

[9] Manfred Diehl, Elizabeth L. Hay, Kathleen M. Berg, "The Ratio between Positive and Negative Affect and Flourishing Mental Health across Adulthood," Aging Ment Health 15 No. 7 (2011): 882-893, www.tandfonline.com-/doi/abs/10.1080/13607863.2011.569488.

spiraled your thoughts into a dungeon of darkness. Our purpose becomes our guiding light, helping you build resilience. You feel more connected to yourself and to others when deriving meaning throughout your day.

We want to cultivate this purpose to enjoy the host of benefits it brings, especially if you are spending time at work and normally feel this mundane sense of emptiness. When you can make the shift to do something more meaningful, it builds your resilience to change, allowing you to be more adaptable in situations. You remember why it gives you joy. Why you chose to be in that industry and the purpose you serve for others and yourself. Coming back to this can be a guiding force to help you.

When we are in these negative mindsets, all our thought processes become narrowed. It is harder for us to see opportunities, be creative, or be in an expansive state. The reason these things become so hard is because what we see is only the negative outcomes. We have already made up our minds how something is going to play out. Therefore, we cannot see the opportunities presented by challenges. This cages people with a closed mindset.

It can also create a victim mentality where we want to complain instead of solving the problem. I have definitely been there. It can be addictive to have these emotions of feeling negative and helpless. You can shift and create change in your life, but only you can do it.

I did this for many years at a previous role. They would not recognize my contributions or pay me for role and responsibilities. I kept pushing forward pleading my case to higher-up management and fighting constantly to speak my truth. I kept getting strung along with empty promises. It became a really toxic work environment. Health issues started to arise. It was not a positive work environment. I knew long before I left that I should have left years ago but I was stuck in this negative mindset - a victim mentality that this is what I was owed.

If I had a deeper sense of purpose at the time I would have realized this role was not aligned. It would have given me a higher perspective and understanding of why these things were happening. Instead of coming at it from a victim mentality, I would have understood that I was out of alignment. When these things happen, it becomes a pressure cooker where something must give. It can create a lot of friction and heartache when we cannot see things from a higher vantage point. Until we are ready to see when we are out of alignment, we can't make the necessary changes.

Our society has not helped in an era of commercialism, telling us we need to be happy by filling our life with more stuff. More stuff to distract us, more things we don't really need but it somehow will give us what we think we need. One of the reasons I went into marketing is to learn how our mind works. How things that we market to people is based on a sense of approval to themselves and others.

The pandemic was a catalyst in a lot of ways, forcing us to slow down. We were constantly consuming, one social event to the next, we kept going at a pace that was not sustainable. Then everything halted. We were forced into isolation with the majority of the population losing their livelihoods, their jobs, their way of being. It gave us a lot of time to start looking inward and reevaluate our lives.

This re-evaluation made us realize how much time we spent working at jobs we secretly loathed. The long commutes we had always done. We realized we could work remotely. We could spend more time with our families. The pandemic forced a lot of people to reevaluate what was important to them. With so many lives lost to Covid, it put into perspective how precious life really is. It forced us to come up against our own mortality.

We can be gone at any minute, so cherish every moment. Many of us didn't learn how to build a relationship with death. The one plain truth is we will all pass on. Most people have pushed or buried these thoughts into a tiny box. One we can put on a shelf for later or maybe never. Death can be a scary thought but also a great teacher. It sounds morbid but our fleeting life is actually a gift. The gift to change directions. To prioritize what is truly important to us.

The pandemic forced a lot of us to realize this is not where we want to be. That life is too short for us to spend most of our time doing something we hate. We spend roughly

90,000 hours at work in our lifetime[10]. Spending that much of our time on something we dislike is not good enough.

That is what we want people to start doing. Questioning. Start being curious about where you are going and why. If money is your main driver, it will never be enough. It is like always being thirsty and never feeling the cool water against your lips. The satisfaction of being hydrated comes from within. Looking within ourselves and going deeper. Filling our own cup first. Understanding our desires, our passions, our why, and our purpose.

You Are Good Enough

You may be wondering, "Why do I need to be good enough to find my purpose?" Because it takes courage to go through a transformation and take steps in a different direction. To pursue your purpose, you are also putting yourself out there. To find the path deep down you always wanted to take but weren't sure whether you could do it. To know you were meant to break from the flock. That is where being good enough comes into play.

Your mind can create a lot of fear shouting objections. All those objections sometimes create inaction. We wish things were different, comparing ourselves to everyone around us and thinking, "If I was in their shoes, things would be better."

---

[10] Dan Cable, "What You Should Follow Instead of Your Passion," Harvard Business Review, November 24, 2020, https://hbr.org/2020/11/what-you-should-follow-instead-of-your-passion.

Everyone is on their own path. It is easy to compare our journey to someone else. Feeling inadequate to their success. Feeling like you are falling short. We are all at different stages in our life and meant to learn different lessons. We are all on our own journey. Comparisons usually don't create positive changes but instead make us feel more stuck. Others can inspire us to create change in our life, but not through comparing our choices with theirs. It comes from an uplifting feeling within our hearts, allowing us to create our own change.

Fear is a powerful emotion, but it does not have to sit in the driver's seat. We can have the courage to go after our dreams anyway. It is scary, trust me. It is not for the faint-hearted, but I know you have the courage to succeed. Even if you feel like you don't. The first part is being curious and open to something better. The second is knowing our hearts need to take the lead.

Our mind has a way of telling us all the reasons why we shouldn't do it. All the pitfalls along the way. Knowing this is key to shifting our focus. Shifting from the fear of doing it to the excitement of what might happen next. Your self-love will help you to calm your mind and move into your heart. When we can trust ourselves and know we are following our path, we can release fear.

When we are following our path from our hearts it creates abundance instead of scarcity. It allows you to move through the fear and keep going. You may think, "What's love got to do with it?" Everything. Your mind comes from a place of scarcity to keep you safe, but your heart will always point you in the right direction. Even when it is illogical to your mind.

A lot of our fears come from our minds telling us we are not good enough to achieve our dreams. Not good enough to find our purpose and follow our path. Self-love is so important on this journey because it will sustain you when you feel lost, confused, or defeated. It creates space to dust ourselves off and keep going.

I am here to tell you that you are enough. You are the beautiful human being meant to be here at this time and fulfill a deeper inner guidance. Sometimes we need to hear it from someone else before we believe it in ourselves. Self-love is not a weakness but inner strength. It will be an important first step of this journey as you embark on finding your purpose.

There may be times when you feel frustrated from lack of progress, confusion, or just not knowing what you were meant to do. That is okay, it is part of the process. Keep going, do the exercises, and keep following your heart. There will be nudges telling you something amazing is coming through your hard work. That you are creating change and a new direction for you to follow your path.

You are reading this book right now because you are meant for more. You were meant to take a different path than everyone else. Follow that light inside of you because it will bloom through your faith and confidence to even walk in the dark. More people are waking up to the fact they were meant to do something different. There is a light inside guiding us when we are willing to listen to it.

I created a meditation[11] you can use daily or when you need to connect to the wisdom of your heart. When the fears are coming up and you want to release it. This meditation can help you have self-love as an anchor and is part of the process of finding your purpose. It will help you keep going, even when the going gets tough. It can guide you through challenges. Know you are on your path and it is unique to you. You are exactly where you need to be. I will be here to help guide you.

You got this! Never forget because this first step is one of many. It is the light and the action you will take that will create lasting change in your life and that will guide you to fulfillment and wonder. You will look back and can't believe how far it took you. Your little feet can take giant leaps, but we all need to start somewhere. So, start here.

Purpose can be that light in the darkness anchoring us in our authenticity. This is one of the benefits of walking your path to find your purpose. To live from a place of authenticity. Once we have a clear understanding of the meaning we create in our lives, it allows us to live from our truth.

It is a foundation helping us to make decisions from a place of alignment. We become clearer with our boundaries in what we are willing to accept in life, while leaving behind what we are no longer willing to tolerate. When we come from this place of authentic truth, we can step into ourselves more deeply.

Purpose can allow us to make decisions with clarity. We become less scared about what others think of us because we have

---

[11] www.fearlesslotus.com/freegift

accepted this new path for ourselves. One that radiates what our soul is here to do. It doesn't mean you will know exactly where you are going in life, but you are creating the steps to lead you there. To move toward being a higher version of yourself. You are taking all aspects of yourself and creating a purpose that aligns with your soul.

The inner work creates a window to see ourselves more clearly. We not only add more meaning to our life but also create a breath of fresh air. We can come from a place of grounded energy when we are making decisions from our heart centre. A place of purpose instead of a place of obligation and fear. We are constantly making these decisions daily whether we realize it or not. It gives us the ability to stand deeper in our truth. We tend to go where the wind blows instead of anchoring in the vision on how to get there. We can't be grounded in our truth if we don't know what gives us meaning. We can stand in our place of love and light to illuminate our way forward.

Our authenticity is what makes us all truly unique. Yet a lot of the time we bend to the societal pressures of what we think we should be doing. We feel pulled to create a life of our own, but we also want to take care of our dependents, or spouses, and our aging parents. There is a shift that happens when we follow our purpose, giving us a new perspective on life. It creates stability we can lean on for support. We can take a stance when it is something we truly believe in. It creates a better understanding of our own life and what truly makes us tick.

A lot of us are afraid to be seen, afraid to speak our truth and stand on our convictions. Whatever they are for you, know that you speak through your purpose. You live through the actions of what drives you. You create the meaning that gives you sustenance. Step by step, the actions you take to live your purpose will create authenticity in your life. It will allow you to explore your own depths. To look inward and start living your truth.

It is a journey to continue to find your purpose and then have the courage to live it. Your purpose may adapt as your life experiences change and refine a new version of yourself. This is how we flow through the rivers of life and continue to refine our knowledge, wisdom, and perspectives. You may find that at some point your purpose might be out of alignment and you morph it into something new. You can come back to this book and redo the exercises to see what has changed over the years. Since we are ever-changing beings, it does not mean this is a one-and-done process. We must be hunters to ensure we stay on track and in alignment with our purpose. The more we flow and become adaptable, the more it will serve us in the long run.

How to Utilize This Book

There is an exercise at the end of each chapter. These exercises are here to give you better insights into yourself and what you may want to create. Your purpose will give you a greater understanding to help you live a fulfilled life. One allowing you to go into the shadows and find the light within. Pulling out the golden light to create a picture of your inner strength.

You could rush through this book and speedwalk through the exercises, brushing past the knowledge that comes in the pauses we take. We want to pause while we read. Reflect and understand the true complexity of who you are as a person. It is in the pause where real magic happens. When you do the work. When you commit yourself to the practices and fill them out to the best of your abilities. The more you pause, the more insights you gain. This is the integration period. This is what creates lasting changes within our life. It can be liberating to gain these insights and to understand our purpose with greater clarity. To adapt and flow to ensure it is with your greatest alignment.

The key is to do the work. This is one of my greatest challenges. I love to consume knowledge, but the real magic lies in practical applications. This can be easier said than done. Some of these exercises can be challenging because the mirror can be a scary reflection. One we look at every day yet tend not to see past the cracked façade below. We brush our teeth in front of it but how often do you go deeper in the reflection? To see not only the light we carry, but also the shadow work. We need to see both sides of ourselves to become crystal clear with our purpose.

Exercise: Setting Your Intentions

A lot of people roll their eyes when we talk about setting intentions. It is a minor step in the process but to be sure, it is a powerful one often overlooked. Where you set your intention is where energy flows. Studies have shown that when we set our intention and build a plan, we are more likely to achieve it[12]. Let's start with the intention and begin to make magic.

- Why have you embarked on this journey?
- What are you hoping to get out of this process?
- How do you want to incorporate purpose in your life?
- Complete the short survey below to evaluate your current state.

Survey:

1. On a scale from 1-10 how are you currently feeling about your purpose?
2. On a scale from 1-10 how do you feel about your career and purpose?
3. On a scale from 1-10 how clear are you already on your purpose?

---

[12] Peter M. Gollwitzer and Veronika Brandstatter, "Implementation Intentions and Effective Goal Pursuit," Journal of Personality and Social Psychology 73 no.1 (1997): 186-199, https://sparq.stanford.edu/sites/g/files/sbiybj19021/files/media/file/gollwitzer_brandstatter_1997_-_implementation_intentions_effective_goal_pursuit.pdf.

What's next...

In the next chapter we will look at drivers creating motivation within our life. When we become demotivated or come up against insurmountable odds, this can help us regain our footing. It can help us build resilience and come back into a state of calm, allowing us to be in the eye of the storm. Building resilience from the challenges we face. We are going to go deeper on this journey and find what makes us tick. What is the fuel driving us, and then we can harness it to overcome any odds.

Chapter 2

Your Why

When I was on the edge of the abyss, going through one of the worst years of my life, this tool brought me back to life. It was incredibly powerful in my healing journey. It helped me find my motivation and drive when for months I had none.

I would wake up each morning focusing on my why. This helped me on my journey. It brought me back to centre. I remembered each day I was here to inspire and teach. Your why is essentially what gets you out of bed in the morning. Your why may be simple. It doesn't need to be complicated. I have found some of the most profound things in our life usually are simple.

Our why is the drive inside propelling us forward. Giving us motivation to accomplish projects, milestones, and excel. It doesn't have to be this incredibly big and audacious concept in our life. We give our why meaning by focusing on what is important to us. That is how it becomes "our why".

Your why can shift and morph as you grow. The experiences you go through mold your perspective. They continuously shape your why. Similar to your purpose, your why is also adaptable. It is the life force keeping you going. The underlying current keeps you moving and can be a sustainable force in your life. It will keep you grounded as you go through challenges. When you understand and utilize your why, it can help to build resilience within you.

My why adapted over the years as I have walked my path. My current why is to inspire and teach. This comes from knowing what fuels me in my life now. Looking back on my career, it was not always the case. I didn't like public speaking at all. I was terrified of being seen. I am an introvert at heart, even though most would think I am extroverted. I am very outgoing but when I was a child, I was painfully shy. I didn't have a lot of friends growing up. I was able to make close connections and then they would move to other schools, and I was left by myself once again. I loved art when I was younger and still love creating because that was my outlet.

I remember my father was trying to "motivate" me in school when I was around eight years old. He said he would pay me money if I got good grades. I am sure most kids would be ecstatic about this offer, but I saw that he was trying to manipulate my actions. This backfired because money was not my driving force. The irony is I chased money for most of my career, and it gave me little motivation. If I knew at the time how to go inward this would have been obvious. Instead, we must stumble in the dark until we learn our lessons.

I started to uncover my why when I began working in insurance. My manager suggested I lead one of the new Employee Resource Groups (ERGs) for women. It was a great opportunity for me not only to step into a leadership role, but also to hone my public speaking skills. We had a lot of events where I would be opening and closing for guest speakers. This was the beginning of uncovering my why.

Our CEO at the time was incredibly charismatic, and leading this ERG gave me the opportunity to spend a lot of time with her. She was passionate about helping women within insurance to succeed. She taught me to be prepared for the unexpected and how to inspire people through my words. I admired her way of telling a story and the passion she executed when she was able to captivate an audience.

We were at the Women in Insurance Cancer Crusade (WICC) event, and I sat beside her at dinner. I told her how inspiring she was to me as a speaker. I wanted to be able to inspire others through speaking. I made a pledge at that dinner to be a better public speaker. Making that pledge to her ensured I would follow through. Even though it scared the shit out of me.

I took courses on presenting and was a member of Toastmasters. I found new opportunities to present at work. I really started to push outside my comfort zone. I realized even though public speaking terrified me, there was nothing more exhilarating than inspiring people.

I started to combine my spiritual practices with my corporate career. The result was heart-centred leadership. I had spent most of my career second-guessing myself, trying to be liked by everyone. I tried to control all aspects of myself to fit into a box I was never meant to be in. Ironically, when I accepted all aspects of my not-so-perfect corporate persona, I gained more respect.

When I spoke from the heart, I would make these profound connections. When I spoke and shared my stories of vulnerability, it allowed people to gravitate toward me. In my spare time I worked with HR to develop workshops helping the employees build resilience and well-being. Whenever I facilitated these workshops, it was almost like a rush of energy would come through me. I became so enraptured by helping, inspiring, and teaching, it gave me motivation to keep going.

When we know what is important in our life, it can motivate us through the toughest of times. Allowing us to become more present in our lives instead of constantly worrying about the past or the future. When we focus on our why, it allows us to be more intentional and centred. All the noise and confusion from our mind falls away so we can be more present.

Difference Between Your Why and Purpose

Your why also is a driving force for you to fuel your purpose. It can be confusing to differentiate between your why and your purpose. Your purpose is what creates meaning in your life. Your why is the driving force for your motivation. It is the pep in your step and your purpose is navigating your actions. Both are incredibly important and are interwoven because of their deep connection.

This is the reason to start with our why as we begin our journey through self-discovery. It can be a great tool to uncover our purpose. It can also allow you to tackle challenges, to overcome adversity and build resilience. When we feel depleted and unmotivated, our why can help us become unstuck. It is the passion we create in our lives. It helps to align and draw on the strength to persevere.

I never thought public speaking would have such an impact on my why. I was so afraid of being seen it didn't even occur to me how much I would enjoy it. The thought of speaking my truth and holding an audience's attention seemed almost surreal to me. Yet I was mesmerized by those who could captivate an audience through their words and energy. I remember watching Brené Brown's TED Talk "The Power of Vulnerability" about how we connect on a deeper level when we have the courage to be vulnerable.

It made me realize how much I envied public speakers. Secretly, I wanted to be on the stage but I never thought I would have the courage to do it. I didn't think I would be good at it. I felt small, and what did I have to say that would mean anything to anyone else? Imposter syndrome undermined my capacity to communicate and downplayed my ability to teach and inspire for many years.

We all go through these moments of fear and overanalyzing situations, wishing they played out differently. We all have these voices inside our heads telling us we are not good enough. Our motivation and drive to overcome these challenges help us to move ahead by leaps and bounds. Yet we need to first walk before we can run.

Achievers of the greatest accomplishments all started the same way. One foot in front of the other. We feel like we need to make these quantum leaps. Our goals can feel far away so we end up freezing. Our motivation completely deflates because we can't see the path forward. That is okay if you are feeling confused and uninspired. You will receive clarity if you are willing to put in the work. Think baby steps. Our why can help us get there. I will show you different practices to help you to feel more motivated to keep going.

Since my why is to teach and inspire, it goes without saying that I love to learn. I think certain people are propelled to learn because they want to share the knowledge. They want others to be supported through tools and resources helping them in similar situations. Usually, teachers love to learn because it fuels their why to teach.

When I started to go deeper within myself and live my purpose on all levels, I wanted to get back into volunteering. I felt drawn to hospice while most people felt uncomfortable around those dying. It called to my heart. I am glad it did because the volunteer training was phenomenal. Training I wish they would teach in schools, so we are more equipped to deal with grief.

It gave me a completely new perspective around bereavement and grief. A deeper understanding of how we try to distance ourselves from grief, sometimes undermining the griever without us being the wiser. Certain phrases are uttered constantly around grief to console people. However, we rarely reflect on whether it actually helps the griever. We tend to distance ourselves from the grieving process, and this also hinders those who are grieving. This experience gave me a better understanding of how to support people in a more meaningful way. It has been an enriching journey filled with tears, empathy, and compassion, but it has allowed me to grow and support at a deeper level.

My purpose is to help people in a meaningful way. Giving back is a driving force in my life. It has always been a part of my purpose even if I didn't know it at the time. At an early age I remember picking up trash on the streets with my mother when she was on the board of directors for United Way. We would volunteer at the events, and this shaped my life in my spare time. It gave my life meaning to help others who were less fortunate. I had spent many years finding areas of volunteering that fulfilled me. I could see at an early age how giving your time to others enriches our lives.

When we can first begin to understand our why and what drives us, it can be the first step in discovering our purpose. It gives us a hint of what gives us meaning in our life. When you create meaning, it will blossom in new and unexpected ways.

We sometimes try to pigeonhole our meaning into something specific. When we weave it throughout our life in different areas, it will create a lasting change. It will help you to engage in all aspects of your life. It can create significance within the tiniest areas and grow into something new and exciting.

As we adapt and grow, so does our why and purpose. Our driver can change and motivate us in different ways based on where we are in life. My why wasn't always to inspire and teach. It was originally to create joy and be fun and fancy-free. It was to have the freedom to travel in my younger years. I used any excuse, mostly for schooling, to see the world. To meet new and interesting people and experience different cultures.

It was fulfilling at the time, and then I found myself wanting to put down roots and find a place to call home. It is what started my travels back to Canada. To be closer to my family. My why evolved to build stronger relationships with my family. I didn't want to see them only once or twice a year.

I didn't want my nephews to grow up and not know who I was. Family became my why and I yearned to be closer in proximity to them and find a place where I belonged. I think that is why I explored and lived in multiple countries searching for someplace that felt right to me.

In truth, I realized it doesn't matter where you live. You create connections and that is where home feels right to you, instead of looking for a piece of land that fits. It is how you live that creates lasting change and motivation. Connection and building strong foundations have always been important to me.

All aspects of our why become powerful beacons because they complement our purpose. The driver of our why and our purpose is the direction or vehicle we are incorporating within our lives. Your why usually complements or supports your purpose. This is something to think about when you start to dig deep within your purpose.

The benefits of your why allow you to create motivation to achieve your goals. It can help you build resilience in overcoming challenges when we are feeling low. When you feel like life has beaten you down. It allows us to dust ourselves off and see the bigger picture.

All these aspects we still have the choices to create change in our life. We can feel defeated by life and let it get the best of us, or we can see the lessons in our situations and our circumstances. We can grieve what has happened to us, but the key is not to allow it to take over. This is not our only story. We need to balance the integration of our circumstances without letting them consuming us. To see a higher perspective.

In times like these I will ask myself, "What is this situation trying to teach me?" This can be easier said than done, but it allows us to see our circumstances as our growing opportunities. To get out of a victim mentality pulling us down. I have been there. When it rains it fucking pours. It can come in powerful waves. The key is to release and let go of our anger. Releasing it will help you to move through the discomfort.

Your why can be a lifeboat when things get hard. It can bring you back to centre even when you are in the middle of the storm and you cannot see the other side. You cannot see through the darkness. It can ground you to keep going. It is a powerful tool to understand and use at your disposal. No matter what the situation presented to you, we have the choice not to let it define us.

It can also help you to stay motivated within your job. When you constantly go through change, restructure, or uncertainty, anxiety and stress can result. These circumstances may be out of our control, but we can choose how to react. When we incorporate our why within work, it can give us more enjoyment. A study found employees whose why aligns with the organization's purpose experienced higher job satisfaction[13].

---

[13] Anja Van den Broeck et al., "Unraveling the Importance of the Quantity and the Quality of Workers' Motivation for Well-Being: A Person-Centered Perspective," Journal of Vocational Behavior 82 (2013): 69-78, https://selfdeterminationtheory.org/SDT/documents/2013_VandenBroeck-Lensetal_JOVB.pdf.

If you want a career that matches your purpose, ensure it aligns with the values of the company. A study found onboarding employees by focusing their unique identity and purpose with the values of the company increased retention[14].

I have worked for companies with amazing mandates, purpose, and values. Yet actions speak louder than words. Pretty words don't translate into trust alone. I saw how their actions would contradict their supposed values. This misalignment created mistrust among employees and a lack of motivation.

A survey in 2024 reported 71 percent of Canadian employees are considering leaving their roles[15]. Find a company that truly lights you up and speaks to what motivates you and your purpose. If you are looking to move to a different company, ask the employees what they really think. This is a great indicator of the type of culture that exists in the company, their true values, and if their actions align.

Aligning your why and purpose at work creates meaning. You become more productive when your work becomes meaningful to you. You want to produce more because it no longer becomes grueling work. Some people will go to work and feel completely

---

[14] Daniel M. Cable, Francesca Gino, and Bradley R. Staats, "Breaking Them in or Eliciting Their Best? Reframing Socialization around Newcomers' Authentic Self-expression," Administrative Science Quarterly 58 no.1 (2013) 1-36, https://doi.org/10.1177/0001839213477098.

[15] "71% of Canadian Employees Considering Leaving Their Jobs in 2024: Survey," Benefits Canada, last modified March 25, 2024, 09:00, www.benefitscanada.com/news/bencan/71-of-canadian-employees-considering-leaving-their-jobs-in-2024-survey.

drained, and others will leave energized because it is gratifying for them.

Another benefit of incorporating your why and purpose is long-term thinking. When you are incorporating meaning into your life you are less likely to focus on short-term difficulties. You understand a higher perspective and the overall journey. This helps you persevere through the challenge. It is part of the path to achieving your meaningful goals and see it as part of the life experience. It is part of your growth journey.

I had a lot of resistance writing this book. There was a lot of self-doubt and back and forth. Yet the idea persisted that if I didn't write my book, my message would help no one. I wouldn't be able to live my purpose of helping people if I didn't persevere through my why to inspire and teach. I would not be able to do that if I didn't see the bigger picture. I needed to understand the self-doubt and that the stories I tell myself are only stories. I can tell a more empowering story. One that can help others and help them break through their own patterns, giving them tools to create amazing transformations.

When we build this resilience through the hardships and boost our motivation it creates a ripple effect. It not only helps our energy, enabling us to complete our goals, but it also increases our confidence. The more we persevere, the more we elevate our ability to believe in ourselves. We have less doubt because we are forging forward. It really is amazing because this concept helps us to spiral upward.

Spiraling up is a positive psychology term allowing one positive to compound on the next. This creates more positive experiences that increase our joyful moments, giving you more energy and positivity to succeed. This is what our why does to propel us forward.

They say if you love what you do, you will never work a day in your life. Sadly, most of us didn't take courageous steps to find what we love or our purpose. I don't think it is because we didn't want to but most of us didn't know how. Self-limiting beliefs can also keep us small. We can fall into a role we think is good enough. Money tends to keep us shackled to the golden handcuffs. Wherever you are on this journey, know that it is never too late to go down the hidden path.

I interviewed Dr. Carolyn Frost (www.healthymindsetliving.com), who discovered her purpose later in life. She is an Executive Coach and Personal and Professional Development Strategist. Her daily practice of journaling helps her move through self-limiting beliefs. As she shared, "I consistently come back to myself and ground into what is true."

Her purpose is to help others recognize what already exists within them. It is a beautiful sentiment since the journey to purpose is often about returning to ourselves. We peel back the layers that hold us back, notice when imposter syndrome arises, and learn to make more empowered decisions.

Carolyn spent a decade completing her doctorate, yet still felt she needed more education. Many of us chase additional certifications because we don't fully trust ourselves. For Carolyn, it was her husband who held up the mirror. He reminded her of the incredible achievement she had already accomplished. She let that truth settle in, and it shifted everything. She realized she was enough. She was worthy of guiding others. This opened a new door to living her purpose and to helping others step into theirs at a deeper level.

Motivation comes from an inherent ability to draw from our inner strength. It can expand the possibilities we see and the opportunities that come our way. When this happens it can feel like magic because there are so many avenues, we can empower ourselves to focus on the things that are important to us.

The power of our why has this ability because it drives us forward. It creates an engine that can start us up and create momentum. When we are lacking motivation, starting with our why can set us up for success.

Our mornings are so incredibly important when we combine this with our why. It is a habit like any other, but it can be the difference between having a productive day or a scrolling day. We want to be thriving not just surviving. I feel more empowered in the morning and during the day when I start with my why.

It weaves an energetic vibration, giving us a boost instead of feeling heavy in the morning. When we are dragging our feet, thinking about all the things we must do for the day, it can create a jolt in our morning routine to ensure we are grounded and centred.

Our why gives us the drive to show up fully not only for ourselves, but for the people in our life. It can create a long-lasting change, allowing us to be in an expansive state. Freeing the mind from the confines of its cage that keep you small by pointing out all the dangers in your way. This gives you a chance to see the sun coming through the clouds. The breeze shifting through the rustling trees is the energetic match to our purpose.

Motivation can feel like bumper cars, gaining momentum and picking up speed only to crash into a wall a moment later. Possibly in the form of another person or self-sabotage, which often tries to keep us safe in our mind so we don't venture out and stretch past our comfort zone.

Infusing something bigger than ourselves within our why can propel us forward. If we are only accountable to ourselves, our motivation can dwindle. When our why impacts others we can guide ourselves to new heights; knowing others will gain from our action can spur us to move forward with impact.

This higher-level perspective helps to create an amplifying why, expanding to our community, to our loved ones, or to the Earth. Others benefiting from our why can elicit action. This new aspect can boost motivation, even when our light feels dim. Knowing the impact we can create helps to build sustainable momentum and habits.

Leadership and Your Why

Your why can help support your leadership. Having a clear understanding of your why can help you be a more authentic leader. When we have a higher perspective of our why it creates a supportive environment, going from a "me" to "we" mentality. We can communicate our why to others by building deeper connections. We can be seen as more authentic, inspiring and fostering trust in others.

I would communicate my why to my staff on a regular basis. They knew I was there to support them and help them be successful. I wanted to inspire and teach because I wanted them to be successful and to shed their fears and doubts so they could be the best versions of themselves at work. For them to be authentic leaders by building a supportive team. This empowered my team and loyalty because they knew I had their backs.

When we incorporate our why within our work, we start to bring more meaning to our work. We start to fuel our performance to a higher level, creating more satisfaction in our job. We also start to have a positive impact on those around us leading by example.

When we are fueled by our why it can break down barriers. We become less afraid of the fears lurking in our subconscious. The higher aspects of your why can give you the courage to keep going. To step out of the mold and lead as your most authentic self.

There are going to be times in your life where your motivation will dwindle. Having gone through that experience I can tell you that you are stronger than you think. Building resilience is no easy feat, especially as creatures who are prone to our habitual ways of being and find change difficult. I am definitely a part of this group. When all areas of our life are disrupted at the same time it feels chaotic. There is no longer one thing you can cling to because at any moment it can change.

Sometimes you have to hit rock bottom to be able to rebuild with a foundation that is stronger than before, allowing your mental state to shift in a different direction. To release the old and allow the ashes to blow away as you rise through like the phoenix you are. Trust me, at the time you may not feel like a mystical bird, but it is true. You are a rare bird. You will look back and understand the weight you were able to carry, the anguish and pain and see something beautiful emerge in its place.

My why was able to give me hope each day. Even on the days I felt very little, I kept going. My mental stamina was depleted but the shifting of waking up with my why gave me a small burst of motivation. It was able to shift my perspective even if it only lasted for a few minutes. It would allow me to see a way forward.

Coupling my purpose with my why has helped me through my hardships. It can be overwhelming and hard but it gives you strength to move through the challenges. To give you meaning when you feel lost in the storm and are not sure which way to turn. It creates a passion within yourself and sets you on a course to continue forward even when the road gets bumpy.

Our why can be closely related to our purpose. There are usually aspects that are weaved closely with one another. Start to think about how your purpose might be related to your why. What is your why actually fueling? What areas of your life light you up?

Your why is the spark and your purpose directs your actions. Both create meaning in your life. If you cannot see it at this point, do not worry. For me, it has interwoven throughout my life, but for a long time I didn't see it. Your why is the beginning step for you to start to uncover your purpose. The exercise below will help you gain clarity on your why. To learn more about yourself at a deeper level.

Exercise: Finding Your Why

The following exercise will help you uncover your why. Use your why as a guiding force in your daily life. It will begin the journey of self-discovery for you to uncover your purpose and start taking action to incorporate it in your activities.

I want to reiterate that your why does not have to be grand or life-altering. Your why is what drives you. Like your purpose, it can be as big or as small as you want. It is what sustains you. Creates the fuel in your life to keep going.

1. Where do you find motivation in your life?
2. What are the main drivers in your life?
3. When you feel stuck, what is the one thing that gives you joy?
4. Looking back over your experiences, what has created momentum in your life?
5. Where do you get the most motivation throughout the day?
6. What gets you excited?
7. What energizes you?

Review your answers and reflect on any common themes connecting to your why.

How can you incorporate your why during your day?

How might your why relate to your purpose? What is your why actually fueling?

What's next...

Let's continue this journey as we explore in the next chapter on our strengths. We will focus on the power we wield with the skillset we have cultivated. We are going to delve deep within our strengths. We are going to utilize tools to gain clarity on our character strengths and how we can utilize them to help us find our purpose.

Keep going, you are doing great!

Chapter 3

Leveraging Your Strengths

We are continuing our journey to find your purpose by exploring your strengths. This can create lasting changes in our life and move us a step closer to finding our purpose. Our purpose leverages our strengths, whether it comes to us naturally or cultivated over years of experience.

People tend to downplay their strengths, especially certain ones in the corporate world. There are certain strengths we see universally, and they tend to be masculine in nature. The rise of Emotional Intelligence has brought acceptance to more feminine strengths. Leaders now see the strength in compassion, heart leadership, and kindness. For many years they were viewed as weaknesses.

We tried to be the stoic leaders eradicating any signs of weakness, only showing strength in its more stereotypical forms. For a long time that was the standard and expected, especially within male-dominated industries I worked in over the years. It is through embracing our true strengths that we can really start to leverage them.

We are authentic when we embrace our strengths instead of trying to emulate other people. They say, "Fake till you make it." I feel when you are faking it you are not being true to yourself. This can also happen when you try to emulate someone who doesn't feel authentic to you. Instead, I suggest being strategic by leveraging your current strengths. Then you are not being fake or unnatural. You can come back to your authenticity and do it your way. There is only one of you with your unique skills, abilities, and strengths. Embrace them!

Don't try to be someone else. I found this to be true when I was developing my skills in public speaking. I embraced my strengths instead of trying to emulate someone I did not inherently align with in my core. For example, I viewed my CEO as this amazing speaker, but her qualities were high energy, incredibly outgoing, and a natural storyteller. Trying to match her energy and outgoing personality would be inauthentic for me. When you are inauthentic, people can feel it. Instead, I compared her strengths with my own and adapted to make it my own style.

I loved storytelling and connecting with people. Not in a big setting but one-to-one is where I shined. To leverage this strength, I would visualize having a conversation with one person. This connection to one allowed me to be fully authentic. I would amplify this feeling to the entire audience. I also had an ability to go first and be vulnerable, sharing stories of struggle and my own misconceived ideas to help inspire others. I had the compassion to understand the struggles of others and how certain topics would resonate with my audience. Storytelling and tailoring to my audience were my strengths. I also connect with people using humour. I would leverage these strengths to create my own magic.

It can be hard for us to fully appreciate our strengths. We have many yet we discount quite a few of them. We may disregard certain strengths based on our upbringing, beliefs, or past experiences. For that reason, we want to start having a holistic approach to our strengths. A deep understanding to help you uncover your purpose. This can be a mix of natural talents with hard work to cultivate our strengths. Clarity in strengths start to paint a holistic picture of how they work together.

Character Strengths

Character strengths can help us build a comprehensive understanding of our abilities. In the early 2000s, a group of scientists travelled the world studying cultures to uncover the foundation of happiness. They found common threads among civilizations with different religions and ideologies, then synthesized these commonalities into twenty-four characteristics, which they called character strengths. They categorized them into six virtues: courage, humanity, justice, temperance, transcendence, and wisdom.

VIA created a free assessment tool to rank all twenty-four character strengths. This is a great way to gain clarity on your top character strengths. You can create a free account and take the test to rank your character strengths and the associated virtue. This can give you a better understanding of your strongest to weakest ones.

This tool can be helpful when we don't have a clear picture of our skillset. It can give us insights into strengths we may not even recognize within ourselves. It also arms us with the confidence to start exploring how our strengths play into our purpose. It can be helpful to see how our character strengths can be leveraged. Another helpful technique is understanding in what capacity or context we use them.

We may utilize a variety of strengths in different areas of our life. To have a holistic approach to our strengths, we need to understand how we use them. How do different strengths play into our ecosystem? For example, you may leverage different strengths with your children versus managing people at work.

We can start to embody all our strengths when we have a holistic picture of how we weave them throughout our day. One of the amazing side effects of working on your character strengths is a higher sense of happiness and engagement. Whether you are working on your top strength or your weakest, it still increases happiness. Either way, your life will be more enriched because of it.

When you understand how you utilize your character strengths, you can cross-pollinate in other aspects of your life. You know how to use the character strength but the situation might be new. This will also increase your happiness and overall engagement in your life.

My top character strengths are love of learning, appreciation of beauty and excellence, honesty, humour, and spirituality. Some of these strengths made sense to me but others puzzled me. When I read "Appreciation of Beauty" I almost scoffed because I thought, "How is that a strength?" I was so biased from the corporate world that I instantly discounted this as a real strength. Don't be fooled by your first reaction. When you start to become aware of how you use these strengths, they become more apparent.

During the pandemic, I would quickly realize this strength became my saving grace. We were living in a condo in downtown Toronto at the time. It had no balcony, no green space, and the shared space was off limits because of social distancing. After a while, my mental state started to decline. Luckily, my partner Jeff was an arborist at the time and considered essential services. I was so thankful for this in so many ways. The fact that he hadn't lost his job, and I was not confined to the condo with him all day. Just me, which didn't bode well for Jeff when he came home. It was like Russian roulette with my mental stability. He never knew what emotional state he was getting when he came home.

One day he found me in a heap by the window, crying. I had reached my limit and was not in a great space. We were in lockdown and couldn't see anyone. We could still go outside but it had been raining for weeks on end. Jeff suggested I come with him to work. He was going to be in a beautiful conservation area surveying trees. He said I could do my rituals and just sit in nature. I protested that I had meetings, I couldn't drop everything to go sit in a forest. He knew when to argue and when not to. This was not one of the times to press the subject but he said the offer stands.

I thought about it a little more. I was torn between my value of being reliable to others and the fact that I was no good to anyone.

In the end, my mental health was far more important. I couldn't be of use to anyone until I was able to figure out my own shit. So, I did what every Canadian does and looked at the weather forecast. It was going to be the first sunny day in weeks and instantly I made my decision. I sent an email to my manager in the US being honest that I needed to take the next day off for my own mental health and cancelled all my meetings.

The next day we stepped out into this beautiful forest at 6 a.m. I will never forget that moment. I smelled the air before the sun started to ascend. In the springtime you can almost taste the dew. I watched the light as it danced through the trees, and I had tears in my eyes. I have never been so overwhelmed by the beauty surrounding me. In that moment, I understood how my Appreciation for Beauty was my strength. It brought me back to centre in a matter of minutes. It filled my heart as I witnessed everything around me as if I were a child seeing it for the first time.

All the worries, anxiety, and mind games melted away in that moment. All the small things I worried about became distant memories. All that mattered was that moment. Completely immersed in nature's embrace. I exhaled deeply. Letting go of everything. Holding on to nothing and just beginning to live and see life through a new perspective. Rooted in stability and peace.

If I had discarded my own mental health trying to push through, it would have been detrimental. It would have taken longer to come back to centre. I knew my mind would have rapidly declined. I wouldn't have witnessed the true power of my character strengths at play. Instead, I would be resentful for trying to do everything for everyone else instead of focusing on my well-being.

Don't be fooled like I was and discount certain character strengths because they don't fit our usual "corporate strengths". Each one is included in these twenty-four strengths for a reason. It also made me realize how I could utilize this strength at work in a powerful way.

This allowed me to create deeper connections at work with my staff, colleagues, and managers. Most people tended to praise people for their work by saying, "Great work". People appreciate praise but it goes a long way to praise the specific skill they excel in. It allows them to be seen at a deeper level. Everyone wants to be seen and appreciated. They want to be recognized even if they can't see their own greatness. When we shine that light, we allow their strength to be illuminated even if they didn't see it.

Recognizing a person's excellence is always key to building their confidence and showing recognition. This gives the person a sense that you understand their skills and appreciate them at a deeper level. It builds trust, connection, and recognition seeing them not for just the work they produce but the strengths they brought to the team.

I went through this exercise when I was mentoring the summer students. Originally, my task was to have a thirty-minute coffee chat with them for two months. It was more of a check-in to see how they were adjusting to the company. Instead, I visualized what they would want from the thirty minutes. I thought back to my first time in a corporate setting coming out of university. I wish someone had taken the time to impart their wisdom from years of experience to me when I was starting out. I thought about the most important takeaways I could offer them. Giving them an edge as they navigated this new terrain and uncharted territory. In essence, I followed my purpose.

Instead of doing the bare minimum, I developed mini sessions. I created fifteen-minute micro presentations for six weeks on the most beneficial life lessons I had learned. I shared different aspects of what I thought would help them excel at their summer jobs but also life skills. Then we would take the next fifteen minutes to have a collaborative discussion on the content.

One of the sessions dived into character strengths. It is an amazing exercise, especially with people you work with. You gain an enhanced understanding of their personality. I asked them to come to the session with their top five character strengths. We mapped them out so we could see how each of our strengths correlated with one another. I asked what surprised them the most and what they learned from the experience. One of the students was relieved when we mapped the strengths, seeing others had similar character strengths. Like me, he had discounted some of them based on what we normally consider to be strengths.

One of the students had love as one of their top character strengths. I told them this is an amazing top character strength. The ability to lead with an open heart is a phenomenal quality, especially when we see leaders leading from a place of fear. Yet love in the corporate world can be seen as a weakness. However, the concept of heart leadership is making its way to the forefront. Leading with empathy, compassion, and kindness makes a lasting impact.

Our strengths help us identify our purpose because they are the foundation for our purpose. Our purpose comes through our strengths, some natural abilities, and others through experience. These strengths will be indicators of your purpose and will propel you on your journey.

When you know your skillset, it can also give you ideas to follow your purpose. Your purpose may still be hazy at this moment. Not to worry, we are in the exploring stages. You are gaining the confidence to keep going, to go deeper and to align with your strengths to create purpose within your life. Whether you are embarking on a new career path, entering retirement, or finding meaning in your spare time.

Your strengths give you a starting point to focus your attention. To gain clarity in the areas where you excel. We usually enjoy activities that we are good at, and this can give you a better understanding of where your purpose lies. We will investigate common threads in the next section, giving you clues based on your strengths to align with purpose. You are a detective taking a closer look at what makes you tick. Gaining greater insights on yourself and discovering your purpose to create meaningful change.

Our strengths usually overlap with our passions. We tend to find activities we really love and come effortlessly. Perhaps not all aspects of our passion are effortless, but the joy we receive in them tends to naturally align with our strengths. Don't worry if there aren't any big burning passions in your life. I found this difficult when I was younger because I didn't really have any big passions. I also thought if I didn't have a passion, I couldn't cultivate one. In school we were taught to follow our passion. Let it be a guiding North Star toward our purpose and what we wanted to do. I agree wholeheartedly with those who have innate passions. Some people are born with an ability to know exactly what lights them up and go for it.

However, not everyone has this ability. Sometimes we find our passions later in life and sometimes we just stumble upon them. It may not be a passion in the beginning. Maybe we just like it and keep going. This was volunteering for me. I always volunteered but I never thought of volunteering as a "passion". It wasn't just the aspect of helping others that gave me so much joy but also the connection with the people I was helping. I wanted to meet the people at the charities and build a relationship with them.

For me it was the emotional connection of being with the people I was helping. Years ago, I volunteered at an organization called Calgary Association of Self Help (CASH). This charity helped people who were struggling with poverty and offered a variety of services including social workers, a soup kitchen, and daily activities to socialize. My favourite activity was running the art class.

I had some amazing regulars who would come each week. I didn't have any real art training. It was more a mishmash of painting and drawing. Jesus and his wife Mary (you read that correctly) would come each week. I always admired them because I knew art was their passion. Jesus was an amazing artist and when I left Calgary, he had painted a watercolour of a horse to say thank you. I still have this memento from him today.

Passion doesn't have to be big or grand, but it does give us joy and makes us happy when we are doing it. It usually overlaps with our strengths and can give us bigger insights into our purpose. It is usually from utilizing our strengths through our passion that we receive so much joy out of it in the first place. Start to become aware of what passions you have in your life. What strengths are you utilizing through your passions?

Your Unique Strength

We have covered many different strengths and how you can discover them to gain better clarity of your purpose. One aspect of our strengths comes from our experience. We may all share strengths but only you have a unique combination of strengths that sets you apart. It is through our journey combining strengths that cultivates our superpower. It gives us our own unique perspective allowing us to see the world in a different light than everyone around us.

I believe it is through our experiences that we start to uncover our purpose at a deeper level. Sometimes we can look back at our life and want to change certain aspects. However, it's these experiences giving us this unique lens that aligns with our purpose.

For example, I worked in the corporate world for eighteen years in marketing. I understand how to communicate with my audience. I have an analytical and strategic mindset, which allows me to see different perspectives. Then I switched gears to learn druidism, shamanism, positive psychology, and energy healing. At first glance they seem like complete opposites. Yet I understood how powerful these practices are in the corporate world. Empowering leaders to be their most authentic self. This gave me a unique life path to bridge these two worlds.

I remember dabbling in spirituality when I was younger, wanting desperately to understand it. Yet those whom I asked about it couldn't communicate in a way I understood. I'm a logical person so it felt like they were speaking a different language. I couldn't relate to what they were saying. I sometimes wonder how my life would have changed if I had switched gears earlier on. Yet I wouldn't be able to communicate in a way that resonates with the people I want to reach. This experience created the bridge.

This is part of my purpose. To be the bridge to help people. Communicating in a way that makes sense to them. People tend to be more open to spiritual practices if they understand the logical side first. It also helps that I was a complete cynic so I can see both sides. It is easier to understand their reservations. To help them open a door through curiosity to learn more.

This dichotomy allows me to see things in a different perspective than most people. It helps me to teach and bring people along. This unique experience allows me to bridge two seemingly different worlds, even though they seem at odds with one another. It gives me a superpower with this unique experience only I have. As one of my friends said to me, "I'm skeptical but I am open to it."

That is all I need, the willingness to be open. A way to help teach people to follow a purpose that calls to them. One that gives them more meaning to help them find the light inside of them. Tools to help them tap into their inner wisdom (we will get into this in a later chapter). To balance the analytical mind with the emotional, intuitive, and creative mind. If I didn't have both experiences, it would be hard for people to walk over the bridge.

Sometimes we have these insights without even realizing it is a superpower. We tend to hide it because we think it might be weird or make us stand out. We may lament being the black sheep or having quirky aspects based on the life we have led. Embrace it! This is not a bad thing. These different elements create your unique identity and the strength that emerges from within.

Think about your unique experience. The path you have lived through your own life journey. What are the experiences that have created your own unique lens? Remember, only you have this exclusive combination lock of experiences. No one on this Earth has the same path as you. That is something to celebrate. Both the light and the darkness. How does this unique strength play into your own purpose?

My top character strength is the Love of Learning because I absolutely enjoy taking courses and consuming knowledge and wisdom. This was no surprise to me at all because I also love to share wisdom. I will give you a hint, if Love of Learning is one of your top character strengths, your purpose likely involves teaching.

Those who love to learn usually enjoy teaching, mentoring, advising, etc. because they enjoy imparting wisdom to others. It is the cycle of helping to educate others on topics of interest. They are usually fast learners or dedicated students of learning. They understand the ways of others and usually enjoy seeing multiple perspectives. They want to understand how people see their views. To constantly adapt to create more wisdom to impart on others.

Those who are amazing at storytelling usually score high on the Love of Learning. Storytelling is another indicator of the teacher path. They want to educate and inspire people on topics that elicit passion in them. It is their way of capturing someone's attention and disseminating information. It creates a connection allowing for those around them to learn through their stories that resonate with them.

Through storytelling you can break down complex ideas and make them relatable pieces of information that resonate with your audience. It increases engagement with your audience and leaves an impact. We have a higher probability of remembering stories rather than strictly facts.

Think about the most powerful speakers, writers, and teachers you've experienced in your own life. What aspects stood out to you the most? When they captivate their audience with their personal stories, it gives a richness to the content. It allows us to resonate and connect with the storyteller, helping them disseminate their information to the world and the message they want to deliver. If this is resonating with you, perhaps your purpose is interwoven with teaching.

Which character strength stands out the most? Have you received feedback on certain strengths over the years? If people constantly point out certain strengths, those are hints pointing to your purpose. Is there a common theme around these repeating strengths?

When you are creating your list of strengths, think back to compliments you brushed aside. We sometimes omit these because we don't believe they are strengths within us. Where have you downplayed certain compliments? Ensure you are not missing any because you don't believe you possess them. Some strengths are hidden under insecurity.

These strengths are absolute gems, especially when it comes to our purpose. When you receive these compliments, don't downplay them. For example, I was told numerous times at work that I can connect with people on a deeper level. I was asked this question multiple times, "Have you ever thought about being a coach?" That should have signaled to me, "Pay attention!"

These comments can be a stepping stone to uncovering a new path for you. Sometimes we don't take to heart the things people say because we don't feel worthy of their praise. Imposter syndrome can also come into play, and it can undermine our own strength because we don't feel we deserve it.

I don't think at the time I was ready to see that path for me. I needed to keep going through other roles until I finally realized how bored I really was, which allowed me to understand why they didn't hold the same luster they once did. We can only see what we are ready to see in divine timing.

These are signs telling you to look deeper. When something is amiss, embrace the discomfort. If we try to avoid it, it can create friction within ourselves. We become tired, restless, bored, and the world around us becomes chaotic. These are symptoms we are out of alignment. Look behind the curtain even if you are afraid. The uncomfortable feeling will only continue when we try to ignore it.

Try to look at all aspects of your position if you are looking to make a career shift. What qualities are currently missing from your job? What are the responsibilities you like and what is draining you? This is adding to your repertoire of understanding what gives you meaning.

I found in my last couple of roles I was doing the same thing. I wasn't learning anything new and the parts I really missed were the teaching aspects. I would have staff I could support and advise but I wanted something more. I missed providing advice on well-being to the employees across Canada. It was nice to hear someone using a practice I taught saying that it helped them overcome a challenge. I missed the human element of my job connecting on a deeper level. I started to feel empty.

Slowly but surely, I felt myself disconnecting. This is your warning sign to make a shift. We need to fully understand our unique strengths to be open to new opportunities. To understand our skillset and how they can be transferable. You deserve to go after your purpose, your dreams, and create the life that truly lights you up!

Our strengths can help build the confidence to go after our dreams. Our purpose gives us meaning in our lives. When we start to live with purpose we create more happiness, engagement, and well-being. Lean on your strengths as you go through this journey of self-discovery. There may be times when you feel unmotivated to do the exercises. You may think your path is already set and it is too late for a change in direction to start something new.

Keep going and remember your strengths will help you persevere. Sometimes when we are demotivated it is because we are pressing up against our comfort zone. This path is not for the fainthearted because it takes work. It takes introspection to places that can make you feel uncomfortable. That is okay, take a break and come back to it. This is a process and the more you inquire, the more revelations you will find.

This book is meant to help you push outside your comfort zone, and that can be scary. We like to stay comfortable because we are creatures of habit. But you chose to find more meaning in your life. You chose to take the hidden path others are too afraid to take. This is what makes you different. You are finding something new because you know something is missing. You were meant for something more and live that truth each day. Take the steps necessary to build motivation and confidence to keep going. You got this!

There is nothing you can't accomplish, and I know I sound like an inspirational poster but it is true. Sometimes we need to hear it, read it, and find comfort in this statement to create change in our life. So many people I speak with are willing to settle. They feel the time they have already put into their career is a sunk cost. They would be wasting time trying something new. They need to wait until retirement, they don't want to make waves, or they feel like this is as good as it gets.

They work in roles they hate and at companies they don't believe in, where they feel undervalued and underappreciated. The role may feel stale or unfulfilling. They spend time doing things that drain their energy instead of sustaining it. Trust me, I know because I've been there. I've worn golden handcuffs and thought I would wait it out. Instead, I got unceremoniously kicked on my ass through a restructure.

When we start down this path to self-discovery it can be transformative. It can start to build your inner confidence and refuse settling. You may be thinking "I have a certain number of years left before retirement. Why would I throw away my security to do something that gives me more meaning?" In addition to all the benefits on living your purpose, there is also the fact that security is an illusion.

We tend to forget this fact. At a moment's notice everything can change. You can be structured out of a company, they could go bankrupt, or they could just kick you out. Sadly, you are replaceable. I also believe when you are out of alignment, certain situations will push you out if you don't make the decision. We call this the "tower moment".

It did not surprise me that I was restructured out of my role, only how fast it happened. I know how the universe works. It said, "Time's up, time to fly" as I was abruptly pushed off the edge of the cliff. Hope you took those flying lessons!

Those flying lessons consist of your strengths. How much time you have spent in the corporate world is not a sunk cost. You have gained skills along the way. You went through challenges and overcame for a reason. These are skills that you can leverage to find something aligning with your purpose.

We have all the tools to change direction, start something new and create a new path. If you hear yourself saying phrases like, "This is good enough," "This pays the bills," or "I just need to get to retirement," it is time to take a closer look. What are you giving up staying comfortable?

When you go after your purpose, know that it is only the mindset we create that is truly holding us back. You can still make financial gains doing something more meaningful for you. There are multiple streams of income that can be generated without solely focusing on your salary.

We tend to think of only the obstacles to doing something different. "I can't do that. There is no way I could change [industries, careers, etc.]". Remember there is a unique set of skills that you have acquired throughout your life. There is no one like you. You are the only one who has your unique experience. You may think the market is completely saturated. How are you different? How can you stand out?

You are the secret sauce. You are the unique human being who has lived your life. This is where inner strength is so important when we are on this journey. It is not easy to look inside of ourselves and know we are worth more. We were meant for more. Your mind will try to tell you differently. It will try to keep you small. It will try to keep you safe, and it will try to make you settle because the fear of the unknown is scary.

You may have heard the 80/20 rule. Success comes from 80 percent of the internal game and only 20 percent of action. We tend to put the opposite into effect. Do more and more until we burn out to be successful. I believe the opposite, and this is one of the main aspects I teach my clients. When we work on self-limiting beliefs and break out of our comfort zone, everything shifts.

Follow a dream instead of staying in a job perceived to be safe. I say "perceived" because there are no guarantees. You could work for a company for years thinking it is a safe bet, only to be let go. Been there, done that. When we combine a powerful mindset with intentional action, it can lead to truly amazing opportunities.

It can be life-changing but it starts with you. You have to make the decision that you are no longer settling. You are going to take the leap of faith to do something different. To follow your own path even when others might question what are you doing.

Don't believe the stories we tell ourselves generating self-doubt. Creating a life where we are making ourselves small. Trying to fit into a box. Instead, the light we each have inside is shining. You have found a new path to follow.

Utilize those skills and strengths so you can find something that truly lights you up. Don't wait until retirement, counting down the next ten years or even five years because you feel like it is too late. It is never too late. It is never too late to find your purpose and start to live it.

Exercise: Leveraging Your Strengths

We are going to do a deep dive into your strengths utilizing different techniques to ensure you don't miss any important elements.

- Analyze your top character strengths from the VIA survey (www.viacharacter.org)
    - What surprised you from the analysis?
    - Could you see where you utilize your top character strengths in different situations of your life?
    - What are you naturally good at and what comes easily to you?
    - What obstacles or challenges have you overcome, creating new strengths out of your weaknesses?
    - Choose five people you trust and send them a message.
        1. Let them know you are reading this book on discovering your purpose and need their feedback.
        2. Ask them what they consider to be your top strengths.
        3. Choose people from a variety of different spheres in your life. One could be a family member, a close friend, a colleague, or a mentor. Each may see a different strength depending on the context of your relationship with them.

- Can you group your strengths into categories or themes to give you more insights into your strengths?
- Are there key themes from your strengths that are pointing you to your purpose?

What's next...

We are continuing the journey to find your purpose. Your strengths and character strengths may have uncovered patterns in your life. This can give you an idea of what your purpose might look like. You may have had some aha moments and revelations as you go through these exercises.

We started in the light with our strengths, now we venture into the shadows of our weaknesses. Our strengths help shape who we are, and our weaknesses are just as important in finding our purpose.

Let's continue...

Chapter 4

Silver Lining to Your Weaknesses

Just as our strengths can hold the key to our purpose, so do our weaknesses. Yet we tend to shy away from them. They can have a hold over us, making us feel like we are not good enough. Sometimes we hide away or distance ourselves from them because it can make us feel inadequate. Most of us were taught to guard against our weaknesses or create a dissonance with them.

Weaknesses can have a hold over us if we allow it. It doesn't mean you are less than or that it devalues your self-worth. Understanding our weaknesses sprinkle additional colour and light to our purpose, while at the same time liberating ourselves from the weaknesses we are meant to overcome.

When we overcome our challenges, our light is able to shine through. We start to shed these old layers of limiting beliefs waiting to be rebirthed, rising back up armed with strength to replace the weakness we shouldered for so long. For us to do this, we need to have introspection. We need to evaluate our lives and see those areas falling short and holding us back.

It takes courage to go within and see ourselves exactly as we are, including our faults and the blind spots. It takes courage to look in the mirror but, in the end, it liberates us. The second part is to not shy away or distance ourselves from them. I am going to show you how to identify your weaknesses, how to embrace them, and how to use them to magnify your purpose.

This is not a one-and-done type of exercise. This is a lifelong journey of self-discovery. Once you are aware, you can use these tools and techniques to transform yourself. To learn more about the various aspects and embrace them. Both your strengths and weaknesses are invaluable to your growth.

I have been on this journey of self-discovery and have embraced the shadows, accepting weaknesses and transmuting them. When you do they lose their hold over you. For a very long time I was trying to control my weaknesses. I thought by controlling them I could keep them at bay. You might not be surprised that this tactic rarely succeeds. Yet most of us were taught this was the best way to overcome them. Unfortunately, it has a reverse effect. This is because you are not releasing it but keeping it stuck within you. It takes an immense amount of energy to control things in our life. When we control and push away our weaknesses, they inevitably start to control us.

We disassociate from our weaknesses instead of compassionately witnessing them. We want to keep them at arm's length. We think if we push through, control, or disassociate they will magically go away. This is not the case but there are techniques we can use. Not only to change our relationship with our weaknesses but to help lead us to our purpose.

When we try to separate from parts of ourselves, it creates a dissonance within us. A blockage because we are not letting it go and accepting. We are in a state of resistance. This exerts a lot of energy because it is going against the flow of acceptance. We separate from our weaknesses or pretend they are not there, creating more friction. It is in this deep surrender that we gain peace, acceptance, and compassion.

The first step is to have a robust understanding of your weaknesses. This takes a level of awareness to first delve into them. We are removing the gap of dissonance from our weaknesses. If you are thinking, "I don't have any weaknesses, I'm perfect!", go deeper and be kind to yourself because we all have weaknesses. We all have shortcomings. How we embrace them is by showing empathy and compassion to ourselves. Our minds can be incredibly critical, speaking in ways we would never speak to others. When you hear these harsh critiques from your mind, replace them with, "I love myself unconditionally."

Resisting and controlling weaknesses is an uphill battle. Instead, surrender to the fact that we are not perfect. We are flawed. That is okay because you can still embrace and love yourself exactly how you are. This is how we align with our weaknesses.

Nature is not perfect. It is perfect in its imperfection. This is us as humans. It doesn't mean that we cannot strive to do better each day. We try to distance ourselves and put up armour around the parts we considered to be our wounded selves. This is how we align with our weaknesses by first embracing them. See them exactly as they are and love them for it. You might think, "How could I possibly?" regarding the terrible parts and the ugly parts in our eyes. Hating ourselves does not help to release the weaknesses, if anything it ties us closer to them.

We can see the full circle of the areas we can release, surrender to, and peel back. We can go within our shadows to see the wounds. To witness our shortcomings, acknowledge them, and build awareness. We can embrace being radically authentic by just being ourselves. Then we can transform.

This wording allows us to focus on a holistic approach. You are accepting yourself exactly as you are. To love yourself unconditionally is a process. For now start building an awareness of understanding your weaknesses and embracing them. Know they are a part of you. That doesn't mean ignoring your weaknesses but using this as a foundation for you to start going deeper. Pull back the layers of your weaknesses and use these insights to bring clarity to your purpose.

The first aspect comes from a place of awareness. We first need to know and understand what our weaknesses are. Then we find the silver lining to our strengths. We do this by first understanding that strengths and weaknesses are on the same scale. Confidence is strength until it goes too far, turning into arrogance. This becomes a weakness. Confidence becomes overconfidence. We ignore advice and collaboration. Employees become resentful if they feel their voices are not heard. Colleagues start to distance themselves because arrogance creates a closed-off mindset.

The silver lining to your weakness uncovers the strength to overcome it. The shift also helps us to reframe our mindset, since we don't want to be associated with the weakness. By shifting our mindset, we are now coming from a place of possibilities instead of only seeing the negative aspects.

If we only see our weaknesses in a negative light, it narrows the opportunities we see. We become frustrated and the solutions diminish. When we see the positive strength, we can open up to more opportunities. You no longer disassociate or resist. It loses its hold over you, giving you the opening to take a different approach.

For many years I was told that I was too emotional at work. I wore my heart on my sleeve. People could tell what I was thinking, or more, what I was feeling. For many years I thought emotions were a weakness. I spent so much energy trying to control them. I tried to disassociate from my emotions at work and bury them. You can probably guess how well that strategy went. The amount of energy I would exert trying to control my emotions was exhausting.

The worst part, I began to lose my voice in the process. I was afraid of saying the wrong thing or they would hear the emotion in my voice. So I wouldn't say anything. Until I was told by my manager that I was still too emotional. I couldn't believe it. I had managed to control every aspect of my emotions. I responded by saying, "But I didn't say anything." His response was, "I could see it in your eyes."

I felt completely disheartened because I felt like nothing I was doing was working. For many years I tried to numb this part of myself in all the wrong ways. I would use alcohol to either feel something or to feel nothing. "You are too sensitive. You are too emotional." I wore these phrases as a badge of weakness. Eventually, there is only so much you can control before it bubbles to the surface begging to be witnessed.

It was only when I started my spiritual path that my perspective shifted. Learning Druidism, shamanism, and energy healing helped me to take a different approach. I realized not everything was black and white as I was led to believe. I realized some strengths are more revered than others. I started to understand the silver lining because I released the misconception people have around emotions.

This shift in my mindset started to empower me. Instead of spinning out of control in the backseat, I finally climbed into the front seat, my emotions riding shotgun. They were now my guiding force, giving me a map to understand myself at a deeper level. They became my GPS to understand how I was reacting.

Instead of judging my emotions, I started to become more curious about them. Too much emotion can be overwhelming. Instead, I built a new relationship with them to empower me. I was no longer controlling but aligning with my emotions. This changed my relationship with them forever.

I am an empath and able to feel people's emotions very easily. Sometimes it can be overwhelming, but it also allows me to build deep connections with people. The ability to empathize is a powerful connector. I could feel what they felt. I could easily understand their desire, what they value, and their fears. Our emotions are also a gateway to our intuition. This allowed me to strengthen my intuition.

This realization changed a huge perspective of how I lived my life. It made me realize emotions can be both a strength and a weakness depending on the situation. This knowledge created the connection. I would leverage the strength of emotions to counter the weakness aspects.

I started to reflect on the positive aspects of our emotions. The most inspiring leaders I have ever worked for or admired had passion when they spoke. They made you feel heard; they had empathy, they supported you and stood up for you with strength. Emotions play an important role in all these aspects of a great leader. So instead of feeling I was too emotional, instead I started to pay attention.

Emotions signal a response, and that awareness allows us to respond differently. Grounding, breathing, and self-awareness techniques can elicit a different response. Asking questions when your emotions take over can shift the neurological pathways. Asking, "What is coming up for me?" shifts you into a state of curiosity instead of reaction. Reflect on your beliefs around your weaknesses. Shift your perspective to see the sliding scale that it resides on. It can be liberating to know that underneath your weakness lies a strength.

Years ago, I had a coffee chat with a colleague named Tiffany. She was a rising star at the company and had proven herself time and again. She confided that despite all her accomplishments; she still felt her education wasn't adequate. She had a Social Sciences degree instead of Business like the rest of her teammates in the division. I could tell the fact that she didn't have the same education made her feel inadequate. That this was a weakness in herself.

I smiled at her and said, "That's great!" She was confused by my reaction. I said, "You have an edge in comparison to your teammates. Yes, they have Business and Finance as their undergraduate. I have taken business, and anyone can learn these inner workings. You have diversity of thought as your silver lining. You studied human behaviour. At the end of the day our business is based on relationships and dealing with people on a regular basis. That is your strength."

I will never forget the brightness in her eyes as a weight was lifted. She finally saw the strength shifting her perspective. It helped her see the value she brought with her unique experience. Sometimes we wear our weaknesses as badges, and they can mentally weigh us down. However, there is always a silver lining to a weakness we can leverage to overcome it.

Transforming your weaknesses can illuminate your purpose by highlighting the strength below. When we can empower our weaknesses instead of being weighed down by them, we can see the hidden gems within. The meaning they create in our lives when we become transformed by them.

Start to think about weaknesses you overcame. This becomes a nugget of wisdom and a clue to our purpose. We usually don't think about our weaknesses to help us find our purpose. However, the lessons from overcoming our weaknesses give us clues to a deeper meaning.

I was terrible at public speaking in the beginning. My shyness would come out and I turned red when people would look at me. I didn't think public speaking would be a part of my purpose, but it aligns. It helps me to inspire and teach and help people lead more authentic lives. I used the silver lining to my weakness to connect with people on a deeper level. I found my purpose and my own authentic flair in public speaking.

While it still scares me and pushes me out of my comfort zone, I still get this rush of energy by living my purpose. I see the sparkle in the eyes of the people I am speaking to and that moment when it clicks for them. They discover a breakthrough, and it has a lasting effect on them. That is part of my purpose and my why that allows me to move forward.

My purpose comes from helping others but also learning and adapting as I move through life. To be open to new perspectives, ideas, and ways of innovation even when I know my mind can be rigid. It is the awareness of this knowledge that allows me to constantly push these boundaries. Not wearing this as a badge of a weakness but understanding that this is part of my path.

Don't let your weaknesses wear you down. Our mind sees things as good or bad. These are relative terms based on society, traditions, and life experiences. Remember, these terms are not absolute. Our minds create duality but in actuality they are on a sliding scale that comes full circle. This mind shift will help you see more solutions, ideas, and opportunities.

Weaknesses help us grow and understand more about ourselves. They are a guiding force and shouldn't be shunned. When we step into the unknown and try new ways of being, we start to understand ourselves better. We can expand our strengths and align with our weaknesses. We're able to walk our path more authentically. It is not an easy task but it is incredibly rewarding.

Pushing outside of our comfort zone is necessary for us to grow. It helps us to gain more confidence in ourselves and our abilities. It is courage that we can use in our arsenal to do it anyway. To show up when we want to hide. To be vulnerable when we want to put on our masks and the shields we have worn in the past. This is how we step into the person we were always meant to be. Not by having no fear, but by doing it anyway. Do the thing that scares you.

Another perspective to help release weaknesses is gratitude. Understanding these weaknesses at one point helped to keep us safe. Our weaknesses tried to protect us in the past. Trying to hide away pain or push others away. Afraid to be vulnerable, we have a fear of disappointment, so we created this dissonance inside ourselves so we don't have to feel it anymore. When we can see our weaknesses attempting to keep us safe, we can build compassion to shift our perspective.

Ask yourself, "What was the purpose of this weakness?" This curiosity opens a door to better understanding, empathy, and acceptance. We start to understand the protective elements. What did it teach you? This becomes important as we continue the pursuit of our purpose.

They are our teachers. A lesson to be learned. Areas we are meant to overcome. We feel shame, guilt, and inadequacy because we struggle with them. They were never meant to be hidden from the world. When we have the courage to embrace these weaknesses, we can turn them into our strengths.

How can we have the courage to see them as beacons of light to us? How our perspective can recognize the possibilities in the face of adversity. They are the areas of the light we need to seek inside of us to be inspired to move forward. Not something to fear.

The humbleness we can carry has magnitude in ways we haven't even realized. They are held in a space creating more room for us to grow. By the growth and experience we share, the strengths blossom before our very eyes. It is through the resilience we hold by understanding it. Giving us the momentum to have an insightful and rich life.

The Silver Lining Model (ACE)

The silver lining or ACE (Acknowledge, Connect, Empower) model is based on the fact that strengths and weaknesses are on the same spectrum. We tend to only see things in black and white. Our minds are designed to sort through information and put them into categories. Start to think about the sliding scale for each strength and weakness. If you have too much of one aspect over another, a strength can slip into a weakness and vice versa. Like in most things in life, we are not aiming for extremes but a fine balance between the two. The sweet spot to tip your weakness into strength.

This teacher we have within our weaknesses is a gift. It is our ACE in the hole. The ACE model has three parts to shift our perspective and gain access to the silver lining of the weakness. We want to align with our weakness to find the strength hidden within.

Acknowledge

The first part of the process is to acknowledge the weakness. We can't work on it unless we are aware it exists. You can analyze past performance reviews and see if there are any common themes. If you can't think of any weaknesses, my suggestion would be to ask your close friends or family members.

Choose someone who you know will be honest with you. Be completely open to their feedback and remember this is part of your growth journey. This is no easy feat. It is hard for us to ask for feedback and receive it with grace. Honour the fact that you are asking someone to share with you.

Ensure you are open to the feedback before the conversation. Set an intention before the meeting. State, "I am willing to receive feedback with an open heart and open mind." This will allow you to be able to receive without judgement.

Secondly, ground yourself before receiving feedback. Visualize roots coming out of your feet and going into the ground connecting with the centre of the Earth. This will bring you back into your body. You will have more self-awareness when you are feeling triggered. It will also allow you to have clarity when receiving the feedback.

Once they have given their response, thank them for their time. Show appreciation for them to show up for you. Now is the time to reflect. Absorb what you heard from them without judgement. See if there are any insights or perhaps patterns you perceived. Absorb their response. Release any negative self-talk your mind may try to create.

Connect

The second step is to connect with your weakness. This can be a difficult step because our initial response is to be separate. We want to create distance and not be associated with it. Instead, we want to embrace our weakness. Accepting all aspects of ourselves. This is part of who you are. If we accept and love ourselves exactly as we are, we are more able to shift from judgement to understanding.

You are also more likely to be in an expansive state. These higher vibrational states of compassion and connection allow you to see more solutions. We can shift our perspective. Uncover blind spots holding us back. We can start to learn and grow. This is an important step in the process. Even just completing this step can help to shift our weakness.

We don't want to deny any aspects of ourselves because this is where we can get stuck in controlling or distancing. I've been there and it won't create harmony within yourself. It will be more frustrating and take so much energy that is not sustainable. It is wasted energy. Trust me.

Empower

As we continue to go through the model, this is where we start to empower our weakness. When we start to shift this perspective to align with the hidden strength. If we look at the sliding scale of your weakness, what are the positive aspects you can leverage? Remember, this also might be shifting your perspective on a strength or a weakness.

For example, one of my weaknesses is being impatient. I want to do a million things at once and I can easily become bored. Firstly, I had to understand the positive aspects of impatience on the sliding scale. It can create desire, motivation, adapting and action.

These aspects helped me to align with the positive facets of impatience.

This helped me to redirect my energy in a more intentional way. To create meaning and purpose in action. To pause and build my patience. I also have other strengths I used to help me to be more patient. My character strength, Appreciation of Beauty and Excellence, allows me to appreciate at a deeper level. When we appreciate, we stop and pause in the moment. It can calm the mind, allowing you to slow down. This combination of strengths helped me overcome my weaknesses.

When we understand how they are interconnected, it can help to create more solutions. We can see multiple ways to overcome weaknesses. This will not only reduce your resistance but also transform them.

This is a powerful model to help you work on your weaknesses and find solutions. However, this is not a one-and-done practice. As one of my Druid teachers said to me once, "This is a lifelong journey, and we are merely continuing to pull back the layers."

So don't beat yourself up if you make progress and then a weakness rears its ugly head once more. Be kind to yourself on this journey. You will be constantly moving through layers of the process, shifting and adapting as you learn more about yourself. Take it one step at a time.

Exercise: The Silver Lining to Your Weaknesses

Identify your weaknesses

- Write down all your weaknesses
- Review past performance reviews and feedback
- Set up three shadow calls to identify blind spots

    1. Identify three people whom you trust and will tell you the truth.
    2. Ask them if they would be open to giving you feedback on your weaknesses.
    3. Let them know you really appreciate their honest feedback. You want to learn your blind spots and weaknesses as part of your growth journey.

Clarity to finding purpose through weaknesses

- What are the unique experiences you've endured to find a path that others can follow?
- Start creating a diary of these experiences.
- What are the weaknesses you are working on right now?

Use the ACE model to work on a weakness

- **Awareness:** List your weaknesses and the opposites of each one (the strength to each weakness).
- **Connect:** Compassionately embrace your weakness. What has your weakness taught you?

- **Empower:** What is the hidden strength in your weakness? What other strengths can you leverage to find your silver lining?

Start to see the spectrum of strengths and weaknesses to transform them.

What's next...

Next we are going to go deeper and explore your values and principles to find your purpose. Think of them as a roadmap. They not only help you find your purpose but also help you to be authentic in your choices. Let's continue.

Chapter 5

Leaning on Values and Principles

As we go through our life journey, values are a driving force helping keep our integrity. Values are beliefs that create the foundation for our behaviours and actions, while principles are rules or guidelines shaped by our values and experiences. They represent not only who you are but also who you want to be.

In Druidism, when we talk about being impeccable, it is guided by the highest version of yourself. When our values align with our actions it creates authenticity. They are the foundation of our being, allowing us to walk through life with integrity.

Having an innate understanding of your values is fundamental for finding your purpose. There are times in our life where we are not sure what choice to make. When we use our values as a guiding force, it brings clarity to what is important to us. They can create the change we want to see in ourselves. Our values are incredibly important for us to be trustworthy to others. We do what we say and mean it.

When our values are not aligned with our actions, it creates inconsistency, evoking negative responses from others when we are out of integrity. We'll all come up against tough decisions. When we have our values guiding our actions, it can help us to stay true to ourselves.

Having a top set of values can help to navigate challenging situations. Especially if you prioritize one value over another. If you are unsure, your inner wisdom can guide you. Feel in your body to help you gain clarity. The term "gut reaction" refers to your intuition. Our values will reflect our body's physical response. You can feel if something is not right in your body. This is a way for you to tap into your intuition.

We can create greater impact in our life by living through our values. They are intertwined with our purpose and can give us greater fulfillment. Our purpose is tied to our unique set of skills that give us meaning. When those are aligned with our values, they amplify within our life in positive ways.

I had mentioned when I first started in corporate, I wanted to try to emulate everyone else. I wanted to be stoic and completely professional and have all of the answers. However, I found most of the time I was afraid to use my voice. Afraid to say the wrong thing or ask a question that would make me look ridiculous in front of others. I was trying to be everyone except myself.

I'm a quirky person, and I thought that is what people wouldn't like or would reject. Yet this is what people embrace the most. The odd and more raw side. When I was myself, my true personality shined through. It allowed me to connect with people in a deeper way. The more I dared to shine, the more meaning and purpose I found in my work. When I started to dig deeper and find my values to live by, it shifted everything. It helped me to navigate a world where corporate politics ruled. There were always two levels being played at the same time.

The more we lean in to our values, the more authentic and trustworthy we become to others. When we use our values to make decisions it creates consistency in our actions. It builds trust and people want to be around others who are congruent with their actions.

When we try to only use logic or self-interest to make decisions, it can create dissonance within us. People can become mistrustful when we make decisions solely out of self-interest. Me versus them. It creates a place of scarcity, disharmony, and distrust. Especially in the workplace. I have had many managers over my career and watched how they managed people differently. I have seen how toxicity breeds when you have a manager making decisions out of self-interest. Taking accolades for the people's work and managing only for their personal gain is disheartening. It also creates a workplace that feels like there is always a hidden agenda.

I have also experienced managers who lifted and supported others. They showed how the whole team excels. One of my favourite managers led with emotional intelligence. He understood that when you lift everyone up, the whole team thrives. He led with empathy, compassion, and support, ensuring his staff was always recognized by senior leadership. He wanted all of us to be successful and to grow and learn. His philosophy was based on abundance: you win, I win. I know he based his decision-making on his values. A lot of my leadership emulated his style, using my values to create trust with my staff. In a lot of ways, it is how I found my purpose of serving others.

I wanted to impart the wisdom I had gained so they could be successful. They could overcome their challenges and find the silver lining to their weaknesses. I wanted to inspire them to release their self-doubt so they could see their limitless potential. I took a heart leadership approach to support my staff. Loyalty is one of my values, and my staff knew 100 percent that I had their back. I wouldn't throw them under the bus because it was convenient for me. I would be their rock and when they had a challenge, I would work with them to find a solution.

Values helped me to stand in my own authenticity in the corporate world. It also created clarity in the places that did not align with me. Sales was one of them. Financial incentive is one of the main drivers in the sales department. This has never been my driver. It didn't help my motivation.

My mother led the business development in the prairie and territories for CMHC (Canada Mortgage and Housing Corporation). She always told me I would be great in sales. I could influence anyone to buy anything. I learned later in life that there was a caveat: What I was selling had to align with my values. If it didn't, I learned I was a terrible salesperson. For example, I was looking after one of my colleague's accounts. It was a large account and there was a specialty product that would give us the edge to win it. I needed to convince one of our underwriters to write it. If he didn't the deal would fall apart.

After speaking with the underwriter, he told me his concerns. He said it was very risky, and he didn't feel comfortable writing it. However, he said he would do it for me. If there was a claim the underwriter would be responsible, not me. I would get praise while losing his respect for putting my own interests above his own concerns. This went against my values. Pressuring him to write a piece of business he didn't feel comfortable writing.

At the end of the day, I would rather him not write the account. If there was a claim, I would lose that relationship. That wasn't worth it for me in the long run. We also shouldn't be taking on higher risk for short gains. I told him if he didn't feel comfortable writing the coverage, then he shouldn't write it.

When my colleague came back from vacation he asked me about the account. I told him the underwriter didn't feel comfortable with the risk. His response to me was, "Why didn't you make him?" I smiled, shrugged, and answered, "Because I'm not built that way." I have watched many people over the years take advantage of people to get what they want. Taking credit for others' work to get ahead. I always wondered how they looked in the mirror at night. Is it worth it? That experience confirmed that sales was misaligned with who I am, and I needed to change roles.

Sometimes we can be great at something. If it's misaligned with your values, you start to feel compromised. It creates a disagreement within you. You start to lose integrity. We all make tough decisions in our life. Each night we look in the mirror and see a reflection of who we are at that moment. Know the person looking back always has a choice each day to show up.

When I was leading the first Employee Resource Group (ERG) with my co-chair, Sheena, we facilitated focus groups. We wanted to make a real difference. We spent weeks hearing their concerns and how to improve. We listened to women across Canada and heard their personal experiences. This is what I loved most about this project. Most ERGs focused on hosting events, but this initiative focused on altering the fabric of the company culture to create real change at a grassroots level. To work with the company to develop a sustainable environment for women to succeed.

When we presented our findings to the CEO, it was a difficult conversation. Our CEO wanted the best for her employees; however, we needed to highlight the areas for improvement. My values played an important role in the meeting. I was representing the employees and had to be honest to convey a unified message.

We worked with HR to craft multiple changes to the maternity leave for people returning. A lot of women felt isolated coming back to work. A disconnect from being away so long with no contact. We incorporated a buddy system to help women integrate with less friction. We also implemented a wellness room that could be used if they were still breast feeding. A lot of these things are standard now but at the time, it wasn't always the case.

The values I consistently rely upon have been loyalty, honesty, and reliability. The combination of these three values is what creates integrity for me, allowing me to keep my integrity when I embody this trifecta. They have served me well over the years. I suggest you utilize your own values. They are incredibly important yet often overlooked. It is usually later in life that we reflect on them. Yet if they are constantly top of mind, we stay authentic and true to ourselves consistently.

Principles to Guide Your Direction

Utilizing a set of principles along with your values can help you to be consistent with your decisions. Ray Dalio, who founded Bridgewater Associates, defined principles as "ways of successfully dealing with reality to get what you want out of life." The more he would learn, the more he refined his principles to reflect his experiences and learnings. They are a guiding force for his company and his way of life.

Principles are an inner compass to guide you to your purpose. When we are bogged down by uncertainty, our principles help guide us to our purpose. You start to see where you are energized and the areas that light you up. Living from your purpose helps to refine your path and gives you more clarity. Each step you take, the universe reveals another. This is how we start to co-create with the universe and find more meaning in our life.

These are my principles to help you understand how I have created a roadmap. This is a flavour of what can help you based on the lessons I have learned. At the end of the chapter, you will be creating your own based on your experiences. They will continue to morph as you are constantly learning. As for these principles, take what resonates and leave the rest behind.

Never give up and be accountable to the people I serve.

This principle is founded under one of my values to persevere. I can be incredibly tenacious to a fault. I will eventually fall and have many times, but I will always dust myself off and try again. I know in myself I will never give up. I love to experiment. I think if I had this as a guiding force at an earlier stage I would have had more resilience.

When I was younger, I had this reoccurring theme of giving up too easily. It stemmed from perfectionism. I wanted to be perfect at everything right at the beginning. I was also incredibly introverted when I was child, so sports didn't bode well for me. I was awkward and weird. Two things I embrace now but not back then. It takes time to be good at something. You need to have the courage to suck before you master it.

If you give up before you even start, then how are you going to achieve anything? When I was accountable to others I accomplished a lot of amazing things over the years. Yet this principle needed to be applied to the areas of my life that really meant something to me. You need to be consistent to see if it pays off in the long run before adapting and starting something new. Consistency helps us to build resilience to stick it out to see where it goes.

I shifted my perspective to focus on the people I serve. I persevere because if I don't, I cannot serve others. I cannot inspire people if I don't show up. I can't help others if I give up. I must be fearless because it doesn't just affect me, but the potential souls I could reach. All the people my message can impact. If you don't shine your light, how can you show others how to shine theirs?

When we are accountable to the people we can help, the people we are here to serve give us more incentive to succeed. I persevere because I am accountable not only to myself but all the lights I can help to shine in the world. It might sound corny but it has served me well when fear has gripped me, or when I was afraid to write, to speak, to share, and be vulnerable. I remember Brené Brown's words, "Someone has to go first." Someone has to the light the way for others.

Experiment and be curious.

Seeing failures through the lens of curiosity as experiments shifts our perspective. Reflecting on what went wrong and how to adapt accordingly. What can you do differently? Every successful person on their journey to success has one thing in common. They all had failures. They had to overcome the challenges and learn from them to be successful in life. We all endure setbacks and challenges but what sets us apart is how you react to them. Do they become your Achilles' heel or are you able to adjust and learn? Move forward with this wisdom you gained to create your success.

This principle helps you build resilience and keep going without attachment to our self-worth. I failed, so therefore, I am a failure. This is not true and reminding yourself of this fact is crucial. You are trying new things and pushing yourself outside your comfort zone. Failure is bound to happen. It is part of life, and this is how we learn. Experimenting allows us to find new avenues to success.

When we are curious it releases the negative self-talk that comes from setbacks. When we are in a state of curiosity we are willing to learn from what has transpired. It opens us up to finding new opportunities and solutions to problems. You learn that these principles can be adapted to help you succeed. Sometimes it is through these setbacks that we create a new principle to navigate those pitfalls in the future.

Does this choice align with my values?

We have defining moments in our life when we look back and wonder, did we make the right choice? Did I stand up for what I believe in? When you look at your daily choices it is easy to follow logic for the answer. Sometimes the answer is easy and other times you can feel stuck. At the end of the day, you need to make the decisions that align with you. When checking in with ourselves, it can help to give us perspective to move forward.

I wish I had implemented this principle earlier in my life. I feel like I stayed at certain companies in my career because it was comfortable. Choosing the devil I knew, instead of the one I didn't. It was not fulfilling by the end and was incredibly toxic. However, I made the choice to stay not out of my values but out of comfort. I thought I was staying out of loyalty but if I had taken the time to reflect on my values, the choice would have been clear.

Our values can help us make decisions leading us to our purpose and path when we pay attention. Combining our values with our principles can help us get there. Leading us on the path we were always meant to take. Sometimes we find it later in life because we are not ready for it. Whichever it is for you, let this be a reminder not to stay in a toxic situation because it feels easier. In the long run change is inevitable. When we make the decision aligning with our values, it can lead to amazing places and give us the courage to take the next leap of faith.

Be consistent.

This one has been a challenge but intuitively I get this message over and over again. I tend to try things but not stick with them to see if they will work out. I start one thing then another and another. I found when I was accountable to work, I would get things done with no problem. Being accountable to myself and my personal goals, however, became a lot harder.

I have applied this practice in my daily life. Routines can help us grow and amplify our progress. I have a morning ritual where I sit in front of my altar and listen to a meditation I created for myself. I can feel the energy become brighter and amplify. I also have an evening practice before going to bed. When we are consistent, our thoughts and actions can create such amazing momentum. When I don't have consistent routines, especially in the morning, then it goes downhill. My mindset isn't in the right place. My self-defeating thoughts will spiral and I am more likely to procrastinate.

I want to reiterate that we don't want to plan out everything. This can stifle flow states and following your intuition. Consistency I am referring to is when it comes to routines that support your growth. These are the ones that help build momentum and minimize the draining habits.

We are so used to being stuck in our minds it can be hard to hear past the chatter. It comes from a place of scarcity. When we align with our intuition it creates an abundance of creativity, momentum, joy, and innovation. Consistency helps to open our intuition in our actions. Being aware of our thoughts is key. Knowing when it is coming from a place of scarcity (our mind) instead of a place of abundance (our intuition). It is a muscle like any other we need to use and flex over and over to start building confidence in our own intuition. The more we follow our intuition, the more it can create amazing opportunities in our life and ideas.

Be open to new perspectives, opportunities, and ways of working.

This principle for me has been helpful in allowing myself to see different ways of working. To be open to new opportunities and to reinvent and innovate. There are two parts of my personality: one that loves to try new things and another that is more traditional. Both these sides can be at odds because when you find a way of working, why would you innovate and try something new?

It is easier to stick with what you know, but we reach new heights when we are open to seeing things in a different light. When we take the leap of faith to experiment, adapt, and tweak. This aligns with my other principle of experimenting. This is on purpose because I want to constantly innovate myself and try new things to see what works. However, I know myself and if I don't innovate, I will try to revert to my comfort zone. This is a reminder to continually grow and expand.

The other aspect of this principle is consistency. Before jumping from one innovation to the next you need consistency to see if it is working. Learn from the data before starting something completely different or a way of working. The key is giving yourself enough time to see the momentum build. Then adapt and learn from the experience.

Why is this coming up?

You may notice certain situations continually manifest in your life. You may see a challenge cropping up in different scenarios but the theme is the same. For example, you may experience financial scarcity. You focus even harder on making money but then life delivers more expenses. Perhaps your car breaks down or you experience theft, creating more unanticipated expenses. You may think to yourself, "Why does this keep happening to me?"

It can feel like a vicious cycle of one thing after another. It can be incredibly draining and demotivating. When these events take place, there is an invitation to go deeper. These situations usually arise when there is something going on at a deeper level. Yet we are not willing to see it in the moment. Start to pull back the layers.

Some experiences may seem completely out of our control. Yet I believe in a guiding force bringing us experiences to learn certain lessons. When we haven't learned a lesson or confront the problem in the same manner, similar situations tend to arise.

We can blame circumstances for patterns repeating in our life. However, when we embrace the wounded parts of ourselves and address them, things start to shift. For me, there have been many wounds around not feeling worthy. Uncovering my own self-worth has been a transformational experience. While we can move through the physical challenge, there is a deeper test usually at play. Both are important but what I have found that makes the most impact is 80 percent internal and 20 percent intentional action.

This question can be profound when we have the courage to look within ourselves. When we start to see the connections to the triggers in our life. No one is perfect and we all have lessons to learn and grow from. It is part of the journey. Most of us find it difficult to go within. For years I kept looking outside myself to find the answers.

We all have internal wounds within ourselves that we are here to heal. Those triggering moments and situations continually find us. This is an invitation to go within to see where we are limiting ourselves. Where are we holding back and where are we dimming our light? This gives us insights to heal and move forward in alignment so we can be more whole and centred.

There are also times when you have done a lot of healing within yourself, and situations can still arise. You might think to yourself, I already dealt with this! Why is this coming up again? Try not to despair. One thing I have learned is some of these wounds are a lifelong journey. Unfortunately, there isn't a place where we dust off our hands and say, "Well, I am done with that. I'm all healed." You may have healed one aspect, but another can show up, saying, "Hey, you forgot about this one!"

This is one of my principles to pull back the layers. To use more probing questions to help understand the root of the issue. To understand why these circumstances keep coming back to bite you in the proverbial ass. As a principle it helps me get out of my own disaster mind. It helps you surrender instead of trying to control the situation. To deal with it in a more holistic way.

At the end of the day, principles help you to adapt and grow. They are guidelines based on your experience helping you to make better decisions. However, they should not be static. Since you are constantly growing and learning, so should your principles. They should reflect the wisdom you have gained to help you make better decisions.

Principles are incredibly powerful when we combine them with our experiences, helping us learn from our mistakes and pitfalls. They are the roadmap to help us to make these decisions. To be more adaptable, resilient, and persevere in the everyday challenges we have to face.

These are my principles, and I am not telling you to use one or any of them. These principles are based on my experience and my journey. Your principles may be similar or completely different. Customize them so they work for you. They can help you navigate pitfalls, overcome challenges, and learn as you go.

Principles can help you on your path of self-discovery. They can create guidelines to find and to live your purpose. When we align our principles with what truly lights us up, anything is possible. A lot of us were not taught how to be resilient, how to use our intuition, how to create and adapt to flow. Principles can allow you to combine all of these elements based on your experiences. Guiding you to your purpose and living through it to create harmony, engagement, and happiness in your life.

The next step is to take inventory of all your own experiences. What are the key lessons you have learned? What were your biggest aha moments? What principles have worked for you? How can you incorporate them intentionally in your own life so your successes can compound? You can create momentum in the goals you want to achieve and start to live your purpose. What are the guiding forces helping you to live in alignment each day? To live from the highest version of yourself?

Exercise: Values and Principles

Now it is your turn to create a list of values that resonate with you. Consider ranking them by what you value the most.

1. What are your top three to five values?
2. How can you use your values to make decisions?
3. Reflecting on your values, is there a common theme that links your values to uncover your purpose?

Next, I want you to reflect on the challenges you have experienced and the success you have achieved. What principles helped you make better decisions?

1. Write down at least three principles that will guide you in making decisions.
2. Reviewing your values, how can you incorporate them within your principles?
3. How might each principle point to your purpose?

While your values may stay consistent, it is good practice to review them and see if they are still aligned. Your principles will also shift as you learn and grow. Your experiences will morph your principles and refine them to better align with you.

What's next...

We are going to explore an incredibly insightful Japanese model to help gain clarity on your purpose. It is a framework that is almost a thousand years old yet still relevant today. This model allows us to shift our perspective and see how our purpose can overlap with four main pillars.

Let's dive in!

Chapter 6

The Ikigai Model

Ikigai is a Japanese concept that roughly translates to "a reason for being" or "a reason to live." The concept of ikigai dates back to Japan's Heian period. Ikigai is about finding value and purpose in life. I have found this model to be incredibly enlightening. I wish I had found it sooner on my path. It helps you to gain clarity on your purpose as well as potential avenues to get you there.

I want you to first set your intention on why you want to find your purpose. Are you looking for a career change? Spending your spare time pursuing your purpose? Are you starting a new chapter in your life?

Does your answer match your intention from the first chapter? Ensure it is aligned with what you originally wrote. If you skipped the first exercise, go back and do it first. You will gain more insights by setting these intentions before diving into this chapter. If your initial response was different, ask yourself what's changed. Was there a shift in your life while you were reading this book? Have your priorities shifted? Make sure you are clear before going through the model and diving into the exercise at the end of this chapter. We want to ensure your intention is aligned to have the optimal result.

The ikigai model is a construction of four Venn diagrams overlapping to give you a deeper understanding of key areas for you to find your purpose. They are "What you love," "What you are good at," "What you can be paid for," and "What the world needs."

There are four overlapping sections allowing you to gain greater insights. The first is your "Passion" created by the sections "What you love" and "What you are good at". The next is "Mission" from the overlapping circles of "What you love" and "What the world needs". "Vocation" is derived from the two overlapping sections "What the world needs" and "What you can be paid for". The last is "Profession" combining "What you are good at" and "What you can be paid for".

The model can seem daunting at first with all the overlapping sections. As we work through the diagram, it will give you clarity and understanding once completed. It can be an incredibly helpful framework to delve into your purpose.

Ikigai Model

What you love

The first aspect of the ikigai model focuses on what you love. This may seem broad, but it will capture all aspects contributing to your purpose. You don't want to limit yourself. Think of everything and anything that falls into this category. Limiting yourself limits your options to uncover new and meaningful insights. This is a creative process, so have fun with it. The more you write what comes to you, the more you'll unlock new and amazing possibilities. Let go of any expectations and don't overthink it. It is time to let your inner child come out and play.

The wheel of life can be a great companion to see multiple aspects of your life. It will help to get your creative juices flowing. Below are examples within these categories that could fall into what you love. Write whatever comes to you. Not everything will make sense. You may gain additional insights later when you analyze the entire diagram. This is a flow exercise so write down the first things that come to your mind.

Money and Finances: Do you enjoy investing, accounting, real estate, or aspects of savings?

Career and Work: Reflecting on your career and work environments, what did you enjoy the most?

Health and Fitness: What physical activities do you enjoy?

Fun and Recreation: What do you like to do for fun? Do you like travelling, cooking, painting, creating art?

Personal Growth and Learning: Do you enjoy taking courses, reading, writing?

Spirituality: Do like meditating, rituals, religious aspects?

Community: Do you enjoy volunteering, attending or hosting events, community service?

Family: Do you love spending time with your children? What activities do you like to do with them?

Think about not only what you love but also what sustains you. Sometimes there are things that we love but they drain our energy. For example, I love watching a ten-part Netflix series on crime and mystery, but I don't feel energized after watching it. Think about what vitalizes and rejuvenates you as you go through this process.

Another way we can go through this practice is to visualize a perfect day. Start from the morning and go through the day. Write down anything that stands out to you. What gives you the most amount of joy, and how do you want to spend your time?

What you are good at

Next on the Venn diagram is "What you are good at". Think about the skillset we talked about as part of our strengths in chapter three. What stands out for you? What do people comment on that you are good at? It is okay if there are things that repeat from the different sections. You want to start to see patterns and repetition as you continue through this process. It will give you greater insights into your purpose.

You can also include things that you are good at but perhaps you don't love. Remember, this exercise is brainstorming. We don't want to limit ourselves. You will gain greater insights with a holistic perspective. It helped me understand where those skillsets can support my purpose even if they're not the main driver.

For me, event planning is something I am good at but don't enjoy organizing. I did it for most of my career because I am highly organized. When I finished the model, I realized this skillset supports retreats, which I really love organizing. I love connecting, learning, and spending time with heart-centred individuals. This aspect resonates with my purpose. It creates meaning in the event space. These skills can always be transferred into something else to support you. All these life skills are part of your toolkit to understanding your purpose.

What you can be paid for

The next section focuses on finances and how you can make money. Think about different professions, careers, and industries where you can generate financial gains. This one can be trickier. If you are getting stuck within this section, AI can help you with inspiration. It can give you different perspectives and innovative roles that are currently emerging. It can help you come up with different professions. You can use AI to see what professions your skillset intersects with your passions.

AI can help in a multitude of different ways to help you generate ideas. Add your answers from the previous sections into the prompt and ask, "Give me the top roles that match these characteristics." You can further ask, "What different professions can give me an edge?" Ask AI to look for any gaps within the industries you are interested in pursuing. Is there a new profession that could fill this gap? Start to think outside the box. Have fun with this exercise and see what comes to you.

Take your time to go through the model. Mull it over for a few days to see if there are other ideas that start to percolate. Talk to your friends and family about it. Are there other professions they would suggest based on your other answers? What areas light you up? Who do you admire? In what areas are they getting paid for their services or products?

What the world needs

This section of the model focuses on what the world needs. What is currently going on in the world? What is happening from an economic standpoint, a health perspective, human rights, technology, and political standpoints? What will continue to accelerate and what is being phased out? Take a bird's-eye view of where the world is going.

How can you make an impact and how can you influence for the greater good? We may think we are too small to make a difference, but everything starts with a spark. That spark can create lasting change. Shift your perspective, what other angles are at play? Have conversations with people to see what is on their minds. What do they think the world needs? How can you create a unique spin on what the world needs?

AI can help you by including prompts like: What is needed in our society? What are the current issues facing our world? What are the greatest concerns in the world? What are the challenges and threats currently being faced by our civilization?

You can include your previous answers for more detailed responses. See what pain points you can ease in our world. Based on "What you love," "What you are good at," and "What you can be paid for," how does this unique experience benefit the world?

What problems can you solve? AI can give inspiration and uncover aspects you may have missed. Think about new and exciting ideas of how you can apply them in the world for the better.

Passion

Passion is a powerful feeling driving people to engage deeply with what they care about most. It combines the sections of "What you love" and "What you are good at". This principle is invoked when we thoroughly enjoy something with the act of skill. This combination ignites passion within the activity. Our experiences create more joy and we continue to learn and grow, either through repetition of the activity or because we are just naturally gifted.

Review these two areas and see what comes to you. What are the activities you enjoy creating in your life? What sustains your energy, and when do you feel vitalized? List all the different areas combining these two sections. Even if you wouldn't consider it to be a passion, you are finding common themes. Our passion can grow in activities through our repetition.

Sometimes we feel our passion needs to take over our life, needing to be this big encompassing emotion to drive us with fearless intent. If this sounds like you, that is amazing and bravo. I have found for myself it can come in waves. Most people I know struggle to come up with a specific passion. When we start from a place of joy, passion can follow. This can take off some of the pressure; you get a smile on your face when you think about it.

Mission

This crossover section combines the two areas of "What the world needs" and "What you love". What are the common themes of what you love to do? How can those activities translate into your answers for what the world needs? For example, I included "the world needs more holistic options to address illness, disease, and mental health". I believe we can heal ourselves. When you combine a holistic perspective, this can help us to heal with fewer drugs. I believe there is a way to combine medicinal practices. As I have gone through my own healing journey, I have seen the limitations of only using one modality. We need to create a new way of living where we can have a balance in mind, body, and soul. How can we create alignment within all planes of reality instead of only choosing one?

From an environmental perspective, I feel we need to learn to build a stronger relationship with the Earth. When we have a relationship built on respect and practicing reciprocity, we can build a better way forward, instead of only seeing it as a one-sided relationship. Gaia and all the spirits of the trees, plants, and flowers are not inanimate objects. They are not just built on taking. Building a relationship means giving and receiving. Finding ways that we can give back to Gaia will allow her to rejuvenate.

We can create balance in our world from the voices of the many. Not those of the elitists who continually take more and more, giving back less and less. The ones who control political systems for their own personal gain. Political structures and governments have already started to crack. Their structures of power and greed are beginning to crumble. Their weapon is fear they use freely to control people. To distract them and to keep them in their place.

As a society we have become so polarized. We can't see each other's perspectives. Fear and hate are fuelling the masses. How can we break this cycle of blame and judgement? How can we come together to solve major issues that are compounding such as homelessness, housing shortages, and exponential costs of basic needs?

Start to see what the world needs through your own lens. What are the areas you are passionate about? What are your gifts can you bring to the world? How do those gifts translate into solutions the world needs? This creates your mission to lead you there. Find alignment through the patterns and insights you gained so far. Keep notes to track your progress with aha moments and insights. These insights might not come right away. It might be in the middle of the night, in a couple of days or weeks. Ensure you are recording them to create a holistic picture for yourself to gain clarity.

Profession

In this section we focus on the crossover of "What you are good at" and "What you can be paid for". AI can help you with prompts by asking this very question to generate different ideas. You can also validate professions you are looking to explore. You can use AI to generate ideas for potential professions. You can rank top emerging professions and see which ones stand out to you.

An AI prompt could include, "Based on someone who loves [insert answers] and is good at [insert answers], what are ten emerging or unconventional career paths they might thrive in?" See what results come back. You may find that there is a hidden niche you could explore as a profession. Try a combination of "What you love" and "What you are good at" to explore interesting pathways.

These prompts can help you to think outside the box for new ideas, products, services, or niche markets. Keep your mind open. What professions excite you? What areas would you be interested in exploring based on your skillset? Remember, you don't need all the requirements for a specific career. You need foundational transferable skills. You might end up in a completely different direction than originally anticipated.

If you are looking at disrupting an industry or a profession, combine your answers to find a new niche profession. An AI prompt might be, "Analyze the current state of [insert profession/industry] and identify hidden or underserved gaps where someone with [answers what you are good at], passion for [insert answers] could create a new niche profession or disruptive offering."

This can be a fun exercise to explore new professions and disruptions in an industry. We tend to think of the same industries and roles we have done in the past. This gives you an opportunity to see what you can create in the marketplace. To understand what is missing and can be filled with your unique experience and skills.

Vocation

When we look at the cross section of "What the world needs" and "What you are good at," we find our vocation. This is where we have the most suitability based on our skillset, experience, education, and knowledge. This section allows you to dive deeper into your unique combination of skills to help solve a problem for what the world needs.

What areas do you excel in that can have lasting impact on the world? Where can you leverage the knowledge you have gained and apply those learnings? Be creative with this section because you may have a diversified set of skills going beyond education. What challenges have you overcome? Are others struggling with a similar circumstance? What did you do to overcome adversity? Is there a process or steps you can replicate to help others in this space?

When I went through this myself, I saw key themes arising from this model. This book emerged through filling a need. I have taken so many courses because I love to learn. Leadership, public speaking, ancient wisdom of Druidism, shamanism, energy healing, and sacred geometry. I realized through all of my studying and experiences there is a need for us to start following our own dreams. I saw two worlds I could bridge with my unique experience. Those who have studied ancient wisdom rarely have the corporate background to communicate in a way that resonates with them. This was my niche.

The ability to see these connections helped me to shape my next steps. How to live more through my purpose by understanding the gaps in the world. Understanding where I fit in with my unique set of skills setting me apart. A lot of people think they don't have anything to give, but we all have our special talents. Sometimes we don't even recognize it because it comes naturally. We don't realize it's not easy for everyone. There are skills we possess that we can teach others.

Some people think this world is too broken for one person to make a difference. I think that is bullshit. One person can set a chain reaction and shift the world. You can call me delusional, but I know in my core it is true. You can make a difference. The world shifts through smaller intentional actions that lead from one to the next. Our actions compound.

Most things that create lasting change started with an idea that grew, adapted, expanded, and spiraled upward. We first need to see this change inside ourselves. We are not powerless. We can make a bigger impact on the world around us. First, we need to get out of our head that we can't make a difference, thinking our contribution would be too small to make any impact. Don't let self-doubt block how you can make an impact.

We tend to think that everything has already been done. We have nothing more to offer. However, no one has the same unique view as you. No one has walked in your shoes. No one has endured the same trials, hardships or experiences in your life. You have a unique set of skills creating something completely unique to make it a better world.

You don't have to create something completely revolutionary. Perhaps taking something and making it better is your unique skill. What the world needs can be seen through the lens of rebuilding what is broken. An AI prompt could include, "What existing processes, services, or experiences in [insert industry] could be made better with my skills in [answers what I am good at] to improve people's quality of life or well-being?"

You are a unique individual, and you have something amazing to offer the world. When we start to reflect and see these patterns on a bigger scale, we all can add our own flavour to make our world better and uncover new solutions.

Understanding the Patterns

This model can give you greater insights into a bigger picture of your purpose. Two things may seem unrelated until you can correlate them to a higher viewpoint. They may weave into one another as you review the sections. You may realize you have multiple skillsets to leverage a new path for you to follow.

As you review your answers, notice repeating information in multiple sections. Coaching, speaking, writing, and teaching came up multiple times on my model. This was a common theme interwoven through all the sections. What jumps out to you? What keeps coming up for you?

When we start this activity you may feel trepidation at some of the key themes. This can be coming from a place of fear. Notice your reactions as you review each section. Our mind can be incredibly subtle if we are not careful. It can try to tell us we can't do something even when we secretly want to. Perhaps we don't think we are good enough or we have a fear of failure. Notice what your mind is telling you as you go through this model.

One of my clients had a major breakthrough after completing the sections. She discovered how to disrupt her own industry through uncovering key themes. It helped her identify where there were gaps in her industry. She combined both her love for humanitarian efforts and delivering value-added experiences to her clients. No one in her industry was doing this and it became her competitive edge. This enabled her to stand out from the crowd while incorporating her purpose. She loves to help support charities and create unique experiences. This process uncovered her hidden talents, cultivating more meaning at work. It opened up an opportunity in an industry that is largely homogeneous and struggling economically.

When we start to write down on paper what we have found, it helps solidify our key findings, whether through writing, visuals, or jotting down notes we can review later. Sometimes there is a lot we write down and if we try to look at everything all at once, it can be overwhelming. If this is the case, look at one section at a time and come back to it. Be thoughtful and take the time to do this exercise because it could have a huge impact on your life, especially if you are taking steps to change your trajectory.

This model can benefit from quarterly or yearly reviews. You can go back and review when you feel a shift in your life. How you want to incorporate your purpose may also warrant a revisit. Perhaps a role or career is no longer aligned, or you are starting a new chapter in your life. We can continually learn from the experience and create a new path forward. This is where magic happens, so this can be a great model that you go back to multiple times.

Exercise: Filling Out the Ikigai Model

As part of your free gift[16] you receive a workbook with an interactive version of the ikigai model. You can use this to keep all your answers in one place. The workbook will give you extra instructions and you can write your answers in the PDF. There is also a video guide in the workbook that gives extra instructions on filling out the model. After reading through the chapter, downloading the PDF, and watching the video, you will have all of the necessary information to best leverage this model.

Follow the four-step process and go through each section, filling it out to the best of your abilities.

1. Create flow state:

    - Turn off any distractions and set the intention for finding your purpose through the diagram.
    - Set a timer and take at least fifteen minutes to go through the model the first time.
    - Follow the nudges, your intuition, and the first things that come to mind as you write in each section.

2. Leverage AI prompts to add ideas to your diagram.
3. Leave the diagram for a few days. Come back to it to see if there is anything you missed. If you have any sparks throughout the day, write them down. Add them to the diagram.

---

[16] www.fearlesslotus.com/freegift

4. Answer the questions below.

After completing this activity, these questions can prompt more clarity for your purpose:

- What stood out to you after completing the model?
- Did you notice any patterns repeated through the model?
- Did you have any aha moments that arose when you looked at the bigger picture?
- What top areas sparked interest for you?
- Do you have more clarity about what you want to focus on?
- What was the major takeaway for you?

Good luck, my friend. I believe in you!

What's next...

You are doing great and I'm so happy you have made it this far! In the next chapter we are continuing the hunt for our purpose. We will delve into starting to live more deeply by embracing a topic most people try to avoid at all costs. They are so terrified of looking at it, they pretend it doesn't exist. But this is not you, you are not like most people because you are reading this book.

So take a breath and let's continue our journey together.

Chapter 7

Purpose Through Hurdles

The story of our life goes through a winding path of joy and pain. It is inevitable that we will endure challenges, which sometimes wreak havoc in all areas of our life. Sometimes we go through so much heartbreak we are not sure if we can endure. Our pain does not define us, it transforms us.

When fires ravage a forest devastating an entire area, it creates space for something new to emerge. Growth begins again and starts anew. The birch tree is one of the first trees to be reborn when a forest is decimated from a natural disaster. While their life span is short compared to the mighty oak tree, it accelerates faster in the early stages. It is one of the first trees to lead the way, paving the way for other trees to follow.

Challenges are something we don't like to talk about. It can feel difficult and triggering to revisit them. These lessons are painful to endure. It is hard not to fall into this place of despair when things start to get really challenging. You can feel like everything is upside down and there is no compass to point you north. It can feel like there is no end to them, but they do help us to grow. We move through these challenges to expand and transform. Each difficult situation we overcome creates a metamorphosis of our skills and strengths.

We do come out stronger on the other end. Sometimes we can't see inside the storm. When we have overcome the challenge, we can reflect, understanding our strengths and the lessons. We see the weaknesses transform into strengths. Witnessing this metamorphosis can allow us to see a new path forward, allowing us to be seen in a way we didn't know was possible.

Challenges allow us to appreciate what we have and our struggles. We can emerge on the other side feeling like a victim or the survivor. The challenges we endure can define us if we get stuck in the circumstances. It can be hard when you cannot see the dawn or there's no ending in sight. Time can lose meaning and it can feel like forever. We can get stuck in the story of "why me?". We can easily slip into feeling like the victim of our circumstances. Trust me, I have been there.

Some of the happiest people I know have gone through some of the most terrible things in life. You can not only survive but thrive and get through it. These experiences change us forever. They crack us wide open to be remade through hardship. This is not to scare you regarding these experiences but to highlight their transformative quality.

This is an invitation to go deeper, which can be really challenging. When circumstances or patterns come up in different situations, it is no coincidence. Some would call this karma. I believe karma is neither good nor bad. It is an energetic force presenting situations in our life to help us grow. When we don't learn the lesson the first time, the situation will inevitably come up again.

When we have the courage to face these wounds inside ourselves, we can slowly start to set ourselves free. This is where our strengths emerge, and new ones are born from these experiences. We are no longer controlled by them and can release the hurt and pain so we can live fully.

Challenges create a sequence of events leading us to our purpose. Hardships have been a cornerstone for leaders to inspire others in perseverance. We inspire through our struggles, and this is how we weave the stories we are meant to share.

There are moments when you feel like you are only trying to survive. This is when it can be hard to keep our faith. When we feel like it is never going to end. It is too much to overcome. Remember, you have survived. You have endured; you surmounted and built resilience through other challenges.

There is a reason the phoenix symbolizes transformation. One cannot be engulfed in flames and not change and morph. A rare bird indeed. The phoenix inspires us to see the beauty in destruction setting the world on fire. Yet it also creates space for the beginning of something new in the ashes. This is the cycle of life. When we innovate, something needs to be destroyed in the process.

We learn the hard lessons so we can make an impact. We are the hero or heroine in our own stories, and through these nuggets we can impart wisdom. A story of resilience usually comes through hard times. I have yet to see someone give a moving and inspiring story that did not have an obstacle to overcome. The story of how it was handed to them on a silver platter does not inspire much. It is not how the world works. We endure and we learn. We create more strengths, tools, and techniques we share with others, giving us hope we can do the same. What we forget is our own purpose can be hidden within the hardship. Our story of transformation can inspire others to transform.

When we face adversity, it helps us understand what is actually important to us. We can become distracted by what we think we want in this world. Our hardships help us reprioritize our life. They become catalysts allowing us to see what is important more clearly. They can bring to light places in our life that are out of balance. They redirect our path to something better. The hardships can force us to create space to flourish.

Finding my purpose involved me losing my job from a restructure. Another area in my life fell away. I could have asked, "Why me?" but I knew the answer. I didn't want to be in corporate anymore. I had always secretly wanted to have my own business. I also secretly knew I didn't want to work for anyone else. I knew in my heart providence would push me off the ledge to make it happen. Sometimes when we are too comfortable, we put off our dreams. We put off where we are really meant to be because there is a part of us that is afraid we won't be good enough.

When we go through these trials, we gain clarity in the darkness. It helps us to see the light once more. There are no certainties in this world. Sometimes life kicks us in the ass so we start living our true purpose.

When we are faced with adversity through hardships, it can force us to recreate ourselves. The structures we create break down, crumbling to make way for a higher version of ourselves. To allow us to see what new innovations can come our way.

Keeping this frame of mind can help us weather through it. The most admired stories are the ones that inspire us to keep going in the darkness, these are usually toughest times of their life. These stories change us, giving us new perspectives, new ideas and ways of being. It gives us a way through to live our purpose to build something new.

Transforming Into Rare Birds

Our challenges open up the doors to new ways of being. The challenges I experienced a couple of years ago were some of the most painful ones in my life. In one year almost all areas of my life came crashing down at the same time. When all the stability you had in your life is gone in an instant, it can be traumatically painful.

Financially we were stretched thin, having bought a house at the height of the housing market. After the pandemic, housing prices soared. It took us a year to find our place that was meant for us. We were also renovating ourselves, which was also getting stressful.

At work, I was dealing with an incredibly toxic work environment. I was running an entire department with lack of clarity, confusion, and gaslighting leadership. My title did not reflect my role, something I had advocated for years. I knew I should have left years ago but I didn't listen to my intuition. Instead, I stayed and continued to endure.

I found out that I was pregnant, which should have been a joyous experience. Unfortunately, it was overshadowed by the fact that I also discovered I had cervical cancer. This was a journey in itself. This was finally the sign that I needed to take a step back from work. Instead of being supportive, they made it a thousand times worse. On top of everything my work declined disability multiple times.

The stress I was under was soul-crushing. It was compounded by being pregnant and dealing with cervical cancer. I was having regular panic attacks even though I never had them before. I cried for days yet still had to work in this incredibly toxic work environment with no support. I felt such deep betrayal for this company I had dedicated so much of my life to it.

Then the day after announcing to our families I was pregnant, I found out I had a miscarriage. The whole experience was absolutely the worst day. The technician at the clinic wouldn't tell me anything. My doctor finally called to tell me there was no heartbeat. I would have to go to the hospital because I needed medical attention immediately. We were supposed to head up north and they wanted me to wait to have the surgery.

After waiting in emergency shuffling from one room to another, they told me I had to come back. It took them three hours to tell me a miscarriage wasn't considered an emergency protocol. I would have to come back in three days for a scheduled appointment. I had reached my breaking point. I told them they could give me the surgery that day or I was leaving to go up north.

It was the long weekend, and I knew in my heart I needed to be in nature. I needed to be in my element, and I needed to grieve.

Hell or high fucking water I was going there. The doctor said that it could be incredibly dangerous if I didn't have the surgery before leaving. Translating to, "If we release you and you don't come back for the surgery, it could open the hospital to a liability." My response was, "I don't care." I didn't care at this point whether I lived or died, which I made abundantly clear to him. I would risk it and damn their policy. Of course, they didn't want the liability so they "made an exception".

The worst part is I was still working while I was at the hospital. I used up all my vacation fighting with work to be granted disability. Since they had declined me, they wouldn't reimburse my vacation time. My family doctor was so appalled by how they handled the entire affair, she said she would fight them on my behalf. She spent countless hours working with the caseworker, trying to understand their innovative ways of declining disability. Yet she was determined to get me this time off. They did finally grant short-term disability weeks later. It was only because she took up the fight herself to help me because there was no fight left in me.

The depression was palpable. There were three months where I thought about killing myself every single day. It didn't matter where I was. If I was driving, I would think about driving the car into the lake or driving the car into a tree. But then I would think about all the people I would leave behind. Not just leave behind but destroy the lives of the people I love. I know my family would blame themselves if something happened. A study found bereaved families of suicide victims were almost three times more likely to commit suicide compared to families grieving nonsuicide-related deaths[17]. A national survey in the UK found 77 percent of participants were severely impacted by suicide[18]. Suicide is heartbreaking and creates a ripple effect.

When I was battling depression, panic attacks, and anxiety, I had mentioned that my why became incredibly important to me. Inspiring and teaching helped me in my career to build motivation. During this hardship my why became one of processing grief and healing. Healing was my why. It became a signal to go deeper into my spiritual journey. I used my tools to heal the wounds left inside me. To help me process my grief instead of trying to numb the pain or push it away.

My aunt has a cottage up north where I spent many weeks in nature. I spent a lot of time in the woods to help me heal. To create rituals and ceremonies to honour grief. A deep connection with Gaia and the elements. I would cry the tears through Grandmother Water. I would ground into the earth. I became well acquainted with all of the elements. Each of my practices brought me closer to connecting back into myself. It allowed me to truly grieve. So many times we hold back our tears. We feel like we cannot allow the emotions to overflow. We see it as a sign of weakness. Yet it is necessary for us to grow and expand. To be in this place, we must first go into the shadows.

---

[17] Jihoon Jang et al., "Risks of suicide among family members of suicide victims: A nationwide sample of South Korea," Front. Psychiatry 13 (2022): https://doi.org/10.3389/fpsyt.2022.995834.

[18] Sharon McDonnell et al., "Suicide bereavement in the UK: Descriptive findings from a national survey," Suicide Life Threat Behav 52 no. 5 (2022):887-897, https://onlinelibrary.wiley.com/doi/10.1111/sltb.12874.

Each morning I would do a morning ritual to reconnect with myself. To see how victimhood evolved and would transition through metamorphosis. To expand in infinite ways even when I couldn't see it at the time. Even when I only felt infinite sadness. We need to be our witness.

To honour the pain and sorrow I was feeling. Even when I felt little motivation, I took little steps each day to help heal the trauma. Even when I felt abandoned, lost, and in complete darkness, I continued forward. I made it out on the other side, but it was not pretty to witness. I felt broken. I felt completely empty inside and a part of me felt dead inside. Your why is powerful. Mine helped me to let go.

The depression medication for me was not working. Anyone who has had to experiment with this type of drug knows it is a long process. After trying different medications, I knew in my heart it was not for me. It was my practices that helped me to overcome depression. Some people find the medication helps and everyone needs to know what is right for them. Instead of medicating, I went into the shadows. I went into the wounds. I surrendered, I healed, and I transformed as the phoenix.

I was also very lucky to have Jeff, my supportive partner in my life. We are both fiercely independent people. He was there for me when I needed him but also would let me go when I needed to spend weeks up north. I also have a supportive network of family and friends who showered me with love. I also made a conscious choice that I would only surround myself with loving and supportive people.

Anyone only taking from my energy, I had an honest conversation with them. If things did not improve, I cut them out of my life. When we go through incredibly challenging and tumultuous times we need strong boundaries. You are already dealing with so much shit draining your energy. The last thing you need are people who only take from you. Remember, we get to choose who we surround ourselves with, so I chose supportive and uplifting people.

While I was off work and healing, I wanted to start volunteering again. Helping people is my purpose. I wanted to find avenues that would help me to bring purpose back into my life. I was on a call with a Druid friend. He talked about his grandfather, who volunteered at a hospice. He was a healer who helped people transition through death. He could take away their pain and their fear. As he told me this story, I could literally feel my heart tugging against my chest. I knew this was where I was meant to volunteer.

When I started to volunteer at Dr. Bob Kemp Hospice there was an opportunity to sit with one of their clients, Suzie. She didn't have a lot of family and wanted someone to be with her. To talk and watch shows with. I absolutely adored her and she had such a sharp sense of humour. She was dying of cervical cancer. The same cancer I had. We watched shows together and laughed together. I held her when she cried when her mother refused to see her in the final days, and I honoured her when she left this world.

I was part of their bereavement program, working with people who had lost loved ones and volunteered with a spousal loss group. I wanted to help those who were grieving. To continue to inspire and teach but in a completely different capacity. I shared my practices with the group to help them heal from grief. I volunteered at their annual bereavement children's camp. A free weekend for children who had lost someone important to them. To hold space for those grieving. I had found my purpose once again in a new setting and context.

Most people find it unfathomable to work with those dying. Yet it was through my own challenges and embracing death that this became my path. It made it so clear to me. Yet a few years ago if you said I would be volunteering at a hospice I wouldn't have believed you. When you realize how much you can endure it makes you want to help others. It gave me the strength to work with some of the most vulnerable people. Supporting them as they navigate the final stages of their life. It is through some of the worst experiences we find a hidden path.

I would go on to work with the leadership team, helping them with their five-year strategy plan as they built the new children's hospice, Keaton's House. I gravitated toward helping the children's hospice because of the miscarriage I had. Unfortunately, it led to multiple surgeries making me incapable of having children of my own. Another hurdle I had to overcome, yet it brought a new purpose to my life.

The volunteer training was intense and lasted almost two months. I have taken over a hundred training courses in my life. This is by far one of the best trainings I have ever received. Everyone should learn about grief and bereavement because we will all experience it.

During the training the facilitator recounted her time at a recent conference on grief and bereavement. One of the speakers had a segment called "Rare Birds". She was referring to the people who dedicate their lives to those kissed by death. She said it takes a special type of person to work with the dying. To help those that are transitioning out of this world into the unknown.

This analogy has stuck with me ever since. Especially when I tell people I volunteer at a hospice. I can tell how comfortable they are with death based on their reaction. Some are completely horrified I do this in my spare time and others in awe. It draws a wide range of reactions, but what I found most interesting are the people who volunteer in this area.

The vast majority volunteer in this sector because they were transformed by death. Either losing someone they love dearly or surviving a serious illness. This transformation has made their hearts want to give back in a way others shy away from.

I believe finding our purpose transforms us into rare birds. It takes courage, faith, and a knowing we were meant for something more in our life. To break away from the flock to find our own path. We all go through challenges creating new perspectives, new strengths, and new ways of being. These experiences hammer down on the stone to reveal your purpose, allowing you the freedom to fully embrace all of your experiences and find a new way of life.

Our challenges transform us because it is through these hardships our perspectives shift. Our lives are disrupted, broken, and re-transformed into a new beauty. Those who embrace these hardships and learn from them become even stronger. Those who wallow because of what has happened to them become stuck and a victim to the challenges they have endured.

The outcome of the worst year of my life empowered me. I could have succumbed to my circumstances and aimed for the tree or the lake while driving but I chose a different path. Instead of choosing death, I chose to walk with death. Honouring the parts of me that had to die, the fears I had to release, and shed away my skin to reveal a new version of me. To scream, to grieve, to honour my emotions, my pain, and my wounds and transform them.

Teaching Through Hardship

A common purpose that comes up often is through teaching. Those who gain meaning through imparting wisdom to help others grow. This purpose might align with you if you enjoy learning and improving yourself. The more knowledge we gain there is usually an emphasis to share this knowledge with others. This could be through mentorship, consulting, teaching, coaching, or advising.

Teaching may be one of your common themes through the exercises so far. You may have gained insights pointing to educating as part of your purpose. Especially if one of your top character strengths involves the love of learning. These are all aspects of those who love to consult or teach, giving them meaning and purpose in their life.

The challenges and transformation in your own life could be a nudge for you to teach others. You may have tools or a framework you developed from your own challenges. This framework could be used to help others on their own journey. Overcoming challenges is no small feat. It can feel frustrating when it has been difficult for you to persevere over a situation. To overcome adversity and see success on the other side. You may feel envious about those who are naturally gifted in these areas. Who can naturally overcome certain situations.

The thing is these people are usually terrible teachers. When something comes naturally it is hard to teach. It is second nature, so they just "know" how to do it. When I've asked someone how they did it, there have been multiple times when I hear, "I don't know, I just did it." That is great for them, but not so great for others who want to learn it.

It is through our disappointments, trial and error, our challenges that help to shape us. It also allows us to build empathy for others going through similar situations. You can feel their frustration and pain because you felt it too. This helps build trust and connection because you have shared these experiences. You can relate to what they are going through.

Embracing your adversity, especially inspiring others to overcome their own challenges, is key. It is your superpower. Not only was it difficult for you, but you also made it to the other side. It is through our challenges that we grow and gain wisdom to impart onto others and help them. To guide and to teach.

One of my favourite quotes is from *The Art of Racing in the Rain* by Garth Stein, "The sun rises every day. What is to love? Lock the sun in a box. Force the sun to overcome adversity in order to rise. Then we will cheer! I will often admire a beautiful sunrise, but I will never consider the sun a champion for having risen."

You are the champion. You persevered through your own challenge and made it to the other side. Own these challenges and inspire others through your story. Know your challenges will help to inspire and teach others. The route you found coming over the mountain will carve a pathway for others to follow. That is a gift that keeps on giving for generations to come.

The Dawn

It can feel like an eternity when we are going through difficult circumstances. Being in the eye of the storm can cast doubt on ourselves, fearing we aren't going to make it through. The pain we go through feels like it will never end but you will make it to the other side. One day you will see the dawn in the distance. You will see the sunrise and feel the warmth on your face once more.

Know that we are not the victim of our circumstances. It can be hard not to fall into this mentality, cursing the things we cannot control. Feeling we have been wronged by the universe. This way of thinking will not serve you. Trust me, I've been there. I have felt angry at the world. Angry at the ripple effect causing a chain-link sequence of events leaving me unable to have children. Yet instead of resisting and continuing to try to control it, I surrendered to it.

When we are out of alignment we need these tower moments. To break through the layers of fear we place around us. When we are too afraid to leave a position, we ignore our intuition telling us it's time to go.

This is why I find it so interesting when I meet people who I can tell were meant to do something different. Their soul yearns for a new path forward, but they are afraid to take the leap. They justify the job they are at because it is "safe". They have the pension, experience, prestige, etc. They have security in their role. However, at the end of the day every job is disposable. I went through at least eight restructurings within multiple companies over the years. In truth no role is safe.

Be aware of this mentality because if you are not meant to be there, fate will find a way to redirect your path. I always knew at some point I would get pushed out because I was meant to do something different. You can call it divine intervention.

At my next role, I was excited for something new. Only to find out two weeks in that I was restructured out of the department I had joined. My manager who hired me was no longer my manager. I was pulled out of the business and into a centralized marketing department. We had zero clarity, resources, or direction. It was the same thing that happened in my previous role and was just as chaotic as the last position. I remember having a conversation with a good friend of mine. I was describing what was happening, and she said, "Oh my God, maybe it's you?"

Some people might take offense with this saying that's completely out of your control. However, I believe we draw our circumstances toward us. It is not because we are good or bad. It is the influence based on the energy around us to shape our reality. She wasn't blaming me for my circumstance but giving me a new perspective. I started to laugh, saying, "Oh my God, I think you are right!"

No surprise to me, the next year I was restructured out of the organization. Some may find this experience incredibly difficult.

Especially the situation I went through two years prior. Yet I didn't spiral because secretly I was waiting for it. I gave myself one hour to be upset and then I was ready to move forward.

A calmness came over me because in my heart I knew I was meant for something else. Perhaps the timing surprised me. I thought maybe I would have a couple more years before branching out on my own, but it was my time. We all have a knowing inside of ourselves. The choice is whether we follow it. It takes courage to take that leap of faith. To create magic in our lives. It is when we are resisting that it can cause a lot of pain and anguish.

So my advice when it does happen, lean into it. It can be easy to slip into the victim mentality but try to shift your perspective. I find it helpful to give myself a certain amount of time to be upset. Scream, yell, and release the emotions that overflow through you. This is important because a lot of us were taught to bury those emotions. They need to be released for the energy to move through us. If not, it becomes stagnant, toxic, and can start to manifest in physical illnesses. Obviously, the length of time for our reactions will differ given the circumstance. For a role that gave me no joy, an hour was enough to release any emotional attachments I had to it.

Once we have gone through the emotional reactions to our circumstance, we can start to ask meaningful questions. What doors might be opening? Ask yourself what the experience is teaching you. What is the bigger picture and what do you truly want in life? What have you learned from going into the shadows and the darkness? We tend to avoid these questions because they can be painful. It makes us feel uncomfortable, but I assure you it will help shed the parts that are ready to be released. What are you ready to let go of to become your own version of the phoenix? A beautiful and rare bird.

Start to think of your past challenges and how you've transformed. Each challenge helps to create strengths out of our weaknesses, adapting our perspectives and learning through these experiences.

As humans we like our habits, we like our comfort and consistency. When our world becomes upside down, we don't know how to deal with it so we usually react. Usually in more destructive ways because it creates uneasiness within us. The continuity of our world starts to break apart. Perhaps the perspectives we held of our life start to shift. What we thought were truths turn out to be stories we told ourselves. In these moments we are more likely to adapt, become less rigid in our beliefs, and willing to see the world in a new light.

It sheds light into the areas of our life that are not working. The things we have put off looking at because it is too hard to face them. Know you will get through it. You will come out the other side stronger for it. You will learn, grow, and be a new version of yourself.

These hardships help us bring clarity to our purpose. It allows us to shift our perspective. We start to see what is really important to us. What creates meaning in our life and how we can live it more fully. The challenges we go through have a way of breaking down barriers to see more clearly the path we were always meant to walk.

Exercise: Learning From Hardships

Journal about the following questions:

- What are the biggest challenges you have overcome in your life?
- How have these challenges shaped your view of the world?
- What wisdom have you gained from going through them?
- How did you overcome these challenges?
- What hardships have shaped your purpose in life or your career?
- Are there frameworks others can follow that you can teach?
- Does teaching feel like part of your purpose?
- How did these challenges change you?
- What did you overcome to get where you are today?

Take time to reflect on your answers. Take in all of the emotions and honour each challenge you have overcome. Release the emotions and let them go back into the ground. Set the intention to let go of the challenges you have faced. Celebrate your wins and how far you have come. The path you have taken and the experiences that have shaped you.

What's Next...

The next chapter can cause some resistance when we are faced with our mortality. However, this can motivate us to find purpose in our life. Let's continue.

Chapter 8

No Regrets

There's a hip hop song by Aesop Rock called "No rEgrets" that I played all the time. When I first listened to it, I didn't pay too close attention to the lyrics. Then as I got older, I found it deeply resonated with me. The song is about a girl named Lucy who was an introvert and spent her life drawing. It starts out with her as a young girl drawing pictures on the sidewalk until one day she stopped. They said, "Lucy, after all this, you're just giving in today?" and her response, "I am not giving in, I'm finished," and walked away.

The song is all about following your passions and your dreams. People thought she was weird, odd, and introverted. Yet at the end of the day, she followed her calling and didn't let anyone hold her back. On her deathbed she said to the nurse, "I've never had a dream in my life because a dream is what you wanna do but still haven't pursued. I knew what I wanted, and did it till it was done. So I've been the dream that I wanted to be since day one!"

When we stop putting off our dreams and ambitions we can truly start to live them. When we look back at our life it doesn't have to be a wish list. All the things we didn't pursue. Instead, it can be a spark that sets us apart. To have the guts to go after it, even when we are afraid. Afraid of failure, of what people will think of us. What we want to accomplish can be big or small, but if we don't try to go after it, a dream is all it will remain.

A worn-out phrase is, "We regret the things we didn't do, not the ones we did." It brings up the haunting question starting with, "What if..." What if I didn't let fear get in the way? What if I had gone after those big dreams I had? What if I took the leap of faith and started my own business? What if I quit my job and went after something that truly meant something to me?

A lot of the time our fears are what is holding us back. It is not ambition, drive, money, etc. These things can play part in what we are willing to do, the risks we are willing to take, but for the most part it is the state of fear. When we are in this fear state it limits our ability to see solutions.

We only see the obstacles standing in our way and we tend to revert back. Finding comfort in the old ways because they are familiar. It doesn't give us this uncomfortable feeling of being vulnerable when we don't know what we are doing. When we try new things, it can be scary because we are stepping outside of our comfort zone.

In the end we want to know we lived to the fullest. We want to know we took all the advantages we were given and made something out of them. We went after our dreams and we took the path that was our own. We don't want these regrets hanging over us. Yet a lot of us still push off what we could do today. We push off those dreams and think, "I still have time, one day."

In the words of Tony Robbins, "The road to someday leads to a town of nowhere." I still think of this quote when I am afraid to take a leap of faith. When I want to retreat and am afraid to fall flat on my face. Afraid I will fail. This is where you catch the thoughts and reflect. It is not true. We tend to think of failure as a reflection of our own worth. Failures are only experiments. They don't define you. The choices you make in this world and the action you take does.

We have so many gifts we are too afraid to share with the world because we are afraid to fail. Embracing this experimentation technique can lead to a new way of freedom for you to try something new. To be fearless and to go after what you truly want in life.

Volunteering at a hospice has been a humbling experience. It puts things in perspective working with terminally ill clients who have months to live. You become more grateful for the people in your life and your health. Death is inevitable, yet we live like we are immortal. Most of us have not built a relationship with death. We are too afraid to look at our own mortality. We push it off or try not to think about it, but death is a part of the cycle of life. It is painful and life-changing.

We only have this moment. Nothing else is a guarantee in our life. If you want to live a life with no regrets, death is where you want to start. There are no second chances once you cross over. So now is the time to start thinking about what you want. What do you want to accomplish? What is most important to you?

This practice may sound morbid, but it can be enlightening and profound, writing your own obituary. That's right, think of your last moment on this Earth. The last breath you will ever exhale. What would your obituary say? What do you want to be known for? What would be the legacy you are leaving?

Reflect on what you have accomplished thus far. This can help you gain perspective on your milestones. The challenges you've overcome. What experiences have shaped you the most? When we face death, it forces us to come to terms with our life. What are the areas we want to improve? What conversations are we putting off? What relationships need mending? In the day-to-day hustle, the most important parts of our life can get pushed aside. We must not only face death but our own mortality. We only have the present moment. The rest of our life has no guarantee for what will happen in the future.

A Druid practice is constantly having death overlooking your shoulder. Not in a menacing way but as a teacher. An understanding that this life should not be taken for granted. The dark angel can actually make us feel alive. Appreciate each breath and be here instead of being stuck in our mind. Essentially, building this relationship can help us live our life to the fullest. We do not forget our mortality and see each moment as a gift. It allows us to appreciate what we have in our life. The relationships we cherish. It puts into perspective the petty arguments with loved ones. It allows us to see what is truly important to us.

It gives us an ability to see clearly what we still want to accomplish. What are those areas that really stand out for you? There is a bucket list we all have, but it is essential. What are the important ones we can start working on today instead of putting them off for tomorrow? Where can we prioritize our own happiness?

Filling our time with joyous moments creating fulfillment in our lives, instead of filling it with tedious tasks of our day-to-day. Becoming obsessed with following the money instead of what truly lights us up inside.

Death can give us a new perspective on life. A couple of years ago, my friend Kelly Campbell lost a good friend of hers. It reminded her how precious life is and it became her catalyst. She quit a senior role in the government after sixteen years to pursue her purpose. Kelly is a Coach and End-of-Life Planning Strategist (www.kellycampbell.ca). She gave up security and the golden handcuffs because she knew she was meant for something more.

It is a moment when we start to see things more clearly. We can start to see past the illusions we created in our life: I have another year, I have this job for the rest of my life, this is it for me. Sometimes we don't act because we feel trapped where we are. This is a scarcity mindset trapping us in a box of our own creation. We can break free, sometimes we just need to turn on the lights.

We always have more options than we realize. Fear, anger, sadness, and frustration have lower vibrational states. It limits the opportunities we can see around us. It is tunnel vision, and we cannot grasp what we have in front of us. The hidden path to something more. It may take sacrifice or a leap of faith. This is where fear gets in the way telling us that we are trapped and stuck.

When we go deeper into a state of surrender, it allows us to see more opportunities. It can give us a way to release the shackles that we have given ourselves to find a new path. To find a better way forward. It takes time and healing, but when you come out the other side it will be more fulfilling. If it doesn't work out, we will find another solution and path forward. It can lead us to something better. Yet when we are in the storm, we can't see the dawn breaking in the distance.

I have been there. When terrible things happen over multiple years, it can be disheartening. I found myself saying, "Next year will be better." Something else would happen and then I would repeat. However, we have the ability to see that this year can be better. We feel like we need to keep putting off our happiness until everything is perfect. It won't be perfect because life is not perfect. Neither are you or me, and that is okay.

We can create situations in our life where we can be happy now. We can go after our dreams. We can find another solution. One of my mentors explained to me, "this is just a moment in time". It does not dictate the rest of your life. We have a tendency to paint the future with the current brush we are using. Yet we have many paintbrushes with a variety of colours to paint something new on the horizon.

The best part about writing your obituary is to know you still get to paint your future. This is not the end but a check-in. You have more breaths inside of you. You have the time right now to live your life exactly how you want it to be. Once you have written your obituary, reflect on your words. What stands out to you?

What stood out for me after this exercise was writing books. It meant something to me to impart the wisdom of all the lessons I have learned and experienced. The fear of writing was overcome by the passion to help people. It was my reminder of why I am on this odyssey. A reflection of my purpose to help others thrive. Finding a new direction on their path.

A few years ago, I kept saying, "Next year I'll write my book." I kept putting it off until I was laid off from my job and thought, "Well now is the time. I have no excuses left, and as I start a new chapter in my life, why not start a new chapter of my book."

We tend to resist what we fear but when we surrender to its loving embrace, we are able to fully see the beauty in death. We can see the transformation that it leaves us with and the moments in between. It is a fully embodying way of being. It is scary because it is unknown. It is a path not chartered until we give our last breath.

In the Druid teachings part of building a relationship with death is to sleep in your own grave. Talk about terrifying! It is an embodiment of letting go of what needs to die. To be rebirthed into something new. It is going through this cycle we transform. Coming into our evolution. Don't worry, I am not asking you to sleep in your own grave, but I am asking you to start understanding your own mortality.

Start building a relationship with death instead of pretending it doesn't exist. I had so much anxiety about my own mortality before I started walking the Druid path. When I started to build this relationship with death, it made me feel more alive. It allowed me to surrender instead of trying to control everything. It made me appreciate all the cycles of life. It also makes you become less afraid of death and our own mortality.

Our bodies and cells are constantly dying and being regenerated. We actually go through this death and rebirth many times within a single day. We just don't notice it happening in our body. It is the nature of life and is everywhere we look. It is not something to fear but to embrace. It is a key to living our lives in true alignment with our purpose if we are brave enough to search for it. If we have the courage to walk a different path than what we have been told. You have a paintbrush in your hand. I am just giving you tools to go deeper on your path, where each day is a gift instead of just a monotonous series of events.

When we give ourselves the space to live our dreams even if we fail, we won't have the regret that we didn't try. Death can be quite a motivator for us to start living our most authentic self. For us to pursue our dreams. If you only had one year to live, what would you do differently? Would you quit your job? Would you travel, volunteer, paint, take up that hobby you always wanted to do? We are only here for a short time in our life, let's make it count.

Death can be the gateway to the present moment. We start to live our lives. We can become more present in our everyday life because now we aren't pushing off our dreams into the future. We are not stuck in the path. We are living now. We are grateful because we are here at this moment. Not taking life for granted is the best way to live. It is the best life we can embody.

Transformation doesn't happen without some level of destruction. We see the metamorphosis of the butterfly and think how beautiful and amazing. That caterpillar literally liquifies its entire being to become a butterfly. We see the change and the beauty at the end, but I'm sure the caterpillar is wondering, "What the fuck is happening?" Transformation is like that and so is finding your purpose.

It is a transforming process that you go through. While it can feel scary to push outside of your comfort zone, you are shedding layers and becoming a new version of yourself. You are going through a death and rebirth. Parts of you need to die to morph into something new. We tend to be stuck in our ways not liking change, but it is necessary. It is no easy feat. But when we accept this inevitability of death it can free us to adapt and flow. This is why our relationship with death is so important for us to grow, expand and innovate.

When we are confronted with death in our life it can also transform our connections. It creates space for us to lean on others for support, understanding the importance of our relationships. It also highlights how our life touches others and our interconnection in the world, opening our minds to perceive from a higher perspective. To see how our lives create meaning through our connections through the people we love and support. Those relationships take front stage.

We start to cherish these relationships more because it reminds us how fleeting our lives can be. How we need to make each moment count. Who we want to spend our time with in this world. We usually gain meaning and find purpose through our connections. How we connect and relate to others can be another element of our purpose.

Our connections are so important because of the meaning they bring into our lives. In recent years loneliness has become a growing concern for the general public. In 2023, US Surgeon General Dr. Vivek Murthy declared loneliness a public health epidemic, highlighting its widespread nature and serious health implications[19]. Loneliness and social isolation increase the risk for premature death by 26 percent and 29 percent respectively[20]. The health concerns are staggering, with the mortality impact of loneliness equating to smoking roughly fifteen cigarettes a day[21].

Death allows us to appreciate the people in our life. Cherish each of our relationships and time together. It reminds us these connections need to be nurtured and supported, giving us the opportunity to start prioritizing them in a more meaningful way. How we want to show up not only through personal connections but also through community.

This awareness of interconnection can lead to a desire to create a positive impact contributing to society or strengthening bonds with loved ones. This connection can lead to our purpose and how we want to start living a more connected life. This in turn creates more meaning in our life. Start to reflect on your own relationships and connections with others. Does this resonate with you as part of your purpose?

When we lose someone we love, it can also create purposeful action. It can inspire us to create memorials for loved ones. You may

---

[19] Dr. Vivek Murthy, "Our Epidemic of Loneliness and Isolation," U.S. Department of Health and Human Services (2023): 1-81, https://www.hhs.gov/sites/default/files/surgeon-general-social-connection-advisory.pdf.

[20] Julianne Holt-Lunstad et al., "Loneliness and Social Isolation as Risk Factors for Mortality: a Meta-Analytic Review," Perspectives on Psychological Science 10 no. 2 (2015): 227-237, https://journals.sagepub.com/doi/10.1177/1745691614568352.

[21] Julianne Holt-Lunstad, Theodore Robles, David A Sbarra, "Advancing Social Connection as a Public Health Priority in the United States," American Psychologist 72 no. 6 (2017): 517–530, https://psycnet.apa.org/doiLanding?doi=10.1037%2Famp0000103.

feel inspired to volunteer or establish charities in their honour. Keaton's House is part of the Kemp Care Network where I volunteer. It is to honour Danielle's son Keaton, who passed away from stage 4 rhabdomyosarcoma at age eight. There are many programs dedicated to children in bereavement. The children's hospice is being built with the vision to provide world-class care and support in a home-like setting.

It was through the heartbreak of losing her son that she dedicated her life to helping other children to receive world-class care. Keaton's House is partnered with McMaster's Children's Hospital to provide holistic care. She has touched many lives through this foundation. It is through our grief and sorrow we can find our purpose and meaning to help others. To honour the ones we love and have a new perspective on life, creating a lasting impact on the world.

Your Legacy

Death is one of our greatest teachers. To not only live in the present but to take charge of our life. To live our dreams with purpose. Our lives are so short in comparison to the world. Those who lived before us. Those who will be here when we are gone. We see the world rapidly changing. Exponentially becoming more erratic with climate change. We are moving so fast that it can feel hard to catch up.

Going through this process gives us the opportunity to reflect on our legacy. What do you want to leave behind? It can be as small as acts of kindness, the impact on the planet, the impact on people's lives, or the impact within your life. What are the lessons and wisdom you want to pass to the next generation?

Do you want to leave the world in a better place for future generations? These are important questions to consider as we reflect on our own life. We can make an impact on this world if we choose to do so. When we are faced with our own mortality, these questions start to arise. How can our legacy create lasting changes?

The more we reflect, the more we understand the life we want to live. This can be important because it gives clues to our purpose. Part of my obituary is to help heal the Earth. I am still not sure what that looks like, but it is something that is ingrained within my purpose. I feel it in my bones, and walking the path of a Druid has a deep connection with the Earth. While the path might not be clear now, I know it will reveal itself with intention. We can co-create when we seize the opportunities presented to us. We can make a global impact for our beloved Gaia.

Without us helping the Earth that gives back to us so deeply, we cannot survive. We have become a society of taking. The indigenous community has developed reciprocity with Gaia. Traditions over thousands of years create harmony and prosperity. Unfortunately, we did not learn these lessons. We did not follow suit, instead we saw the Earth as an inanimate object ripe for the picking.

I want to make a difference so we can create a sustainable future for generations after us. I don't have all the answers, but I know this is part of my path. My intention is to walk in harmony with the Earth, to raise awareness, and be more sustainable. As we move through the next level of our own evolution, how can we create a world our children can be proud of inheriting?

Start to think about your own legacy. What is important to you? What areas of your life do you want to focus on? Each person has their own answer and their own legacy to create. Ensure it is something meaningful to you. When it is important, you are more likely to take the time to weave it into your life.

As you go through the process of writing your obituary, think about your legacy. A lot of us get a great sense of purpose when we are serving others. Doing what we love and being in service to others can create a meaningful sense of purpose.

When we come face-to-face with the hard truth of our mortality, it shifts perspectives. We can start to free ourselves to become more alive. We can gain so much clarity when we appreciate what we have. We tend to forget about our own mortality. Waiting and putting things off for another day. We place it in our "one day" file, filing away our dreams.

We may not realize it but we are constantly going through the death process. We finish projects, we close relationships, we release old versions of ourselves, and we start again. Death allows us to create new beginnings in our life. It is the natural release we will follow from this life to the next. When we are no longer afraid of this part of the cycle we can gain insightful wisdom. We can live in the moment and appreciate the process and the journey of our life.

What are your priorities that have not been given proper attention? The people in your life whom you want to build stronger relationships with and cherish? What is your unwritten story that you want to experience? Writing our obituary highlights these aspects and gives us the opportunity to still write and live them.

When I did this exercise, helping and inspiring people came through in multiple ways. Volunteering at the hospice, workshops I wanted to create, coaching, writing books to help people live fulfilling lives. All these areas were clues to help me understand my purpose more deeply. Prioritizing the different areas where I wanted to fulfill my purpose. This is my legacy and how I want to be remembered when I die. To be a lighthouse in the darkness. To help and support others. What are the common themes and threads you see through your purpose?

The best part about this exercise is that you have time. You can take the necessary steps to live your purpose. To start acting on what you want to accomplish. Don't put it off and have regrets. Even if they are tiny steps, they will still take you where you need to go. The hardest part is starting. It can be daunting but once you begin, it will create a rewarding journey.

Exercise: Writing Your Obituary

You now have a better understanding of the importance of building a relationship with death and finding your purpose. Now is the time to embrace it. You are going to write your own obituary. Out of all the exercises, this one might pose the most resistance. I get it. It took a while for me to write my own obituary. Facing our mortality can be daunting. However, it will give you amazing insights. Not only to your purpose but to what is important to you.

This is profound in understanding and prioritizing the areas of your life that mean the most to you. It helps to give you clarity and focus. It can give you a better idea of the areas of your life you want to spend more time developing. It can also tell you what is still left that you want to accomplish. This practice gives you an idea of what you really want to pursue. It can also give you a better idea of the themes that come up while writing your obituary. Review each part of your obituary including your accomplishments, milestones, challenges you've overcome, and what you still want to accomplish.

After writing your obituary, review and reflect on the following questions:

- What are the emotions you feel when you read what you wrote?
- What stands out the most for you?
- What are those dreams that still have not been realized?
- How can you start to take baby steps toward them?
- Who are the people in your life that you want to spend more time with and nurture those relationships?

- Do you see your purpose come through your obituary?
- What is the light that shines through as you wrote your obituary?

What's Next...

You have been doing an amazing job working through each of the exercises, which I know takes time. It can be easy to blow through a book and read it quickly. To really understand your purpose, you need to put in the work and dive deeper. This last one can be a hard one to complete, so I congratulate you on your perseverance. In the next chapter we will review everything. Delve into the key learnings from the lessons to give you a clear idea of what you can peruse to give your life more engagement and meaning to you.

Chapter 9

Clarity in Purpose

You have had tremendous courage to make it this far. Building self-awareness and understanding the multi-dimensions of yourself. Pushing outside your comfort zone by asking for feedback on your weaknesses. Writing your obituary and contemplating your own mortality is not for the faint of heart. It is courage you have displayed that got you to this point. The courage to do the exercises and see yourself in the mirror.

When I started going into this deep work years ago, I didn't fully realize how hard it can be. It is still not easy to peel back the layers. Yet when we own these wounds and release them, it creates empowerment. We open up to curiosity, an invitation to go deeper. You are the creator of your own reality, and this is where we are going to take it up a notch.

We are going to explore the patterns and themes to bring clarity to your purpose. I'm also going to teach you intuitive techniques to tap into your inner wisdom. This will give you deeper insight into your purpose.

Each chapter and exercise is a clue to the puzzle to better understand what truly lights you up. How you can start building this into your life. You may have already found your purpose based on these exercises. In case you are still unsure we will go through what the patterns may look like. What is the key theme and most importantly, what you learned about yourself. This work can give us a better understanding of who we are as a person. This can help us to find our purpose but also to speak our truth.

Purpose allows us to gain more meaning doing the things we find enjoyable. Our soul resonates with the activities giving us joy, creating a deeper meaning for us to build motivation, our joy, and our engagement. When we are living our purpose there is a resonance with our soul creating harmony within us. We are living our purpose with authenticity because it aligns with us. Our purpose may adapt the older we get and what stage of life we are in. We may find one part of our purpose leads to another. It adapts and morphs as we learn and grow.

Our Why

Understanding "our why" helps us to gain more passion and clarity to finding our purpose. Our why is slightly different than our purpose. These two concepts complement one another. "Your why" propels you forward. It helps sustain your motivation and elicits your passion. It is a driving force in your life. I had also mentioned it does not have to be a big grand affair to be "your why". It doesn't have to be life-changing but it does have to resonate with you.

"Our why" can give us insights into our purpose because they are closely linked. "My why" is to teach and inspire, which drives me each day. My purpose is to help others and be a guide for them on their journey. "A walker" as the trees would call me because I walk with people on their path. Yet my motivation or why comes from the inspiration I can give to help people transform. To teach them the knowledge I have learned. The result of "my why" is my purpose.

Start to see if you can build a connection between these two concepts. Are there any aha moments when you started to connect "your why" to your purpose? Are there any linking themes you can see with "your why" to help gain more clarity on your purpose?

Strengths

We continued our journey exploring your strengths. We explored not only the strengths you are aware of but also your character strengths. After completing the VIA survey, they will send you a ranking of your twenty-four character strengths, from your strongest to your weakest, with your top five signature strengths. When you reviewed the ranking, did any strengths surprise you? Any strengths you may have dismissed?

Think back to when others commented on your talents. This feedback can be invaluable when we are discovering our purpose. Especially if we don't see it in ourselves. Sometimes we only see past strengths not new strengths emerging from the darkness. Each aspect of yourself is a clue to your purpose. It gives you the ability to understand how you can contribute your purpose to the world.

Our strengths help us uncover our purpose because we usually utilize them as part of our purpose. It gives us more fulfillment to be utilizing our strengths. It creates more engagement and meaning in our life. When you look at your top five character strengths, are there any patterns you see in connection with your purpose?

Weaknesses

We delved into our weaknesses and how to turn them into strengths. We used the Silver Lining Technique to overcome weaknesses, focusing on embracing them instead of pushing them away. When we no longer try to control them, we can start to shift and transform. Aligning with our weaknesses helps us turn them into our strengths and releases the weight they carry when we try to disassociate from them.

As part of the exercise, you were tasked to have three shadow calls. This is no easy task. Yet this is important for our growth and discovering our purpose. We all have blind spots. Some we are aware of and some we aren't. When we can gain insight from others close to us, they can shine a light on areas that might be holding us back.

After summarizing your weaknesses and reviewing those you have now turned into strengths, answer these questions: How has it compared to what you thought were your original strengths? Are there similarities or themes you see emerging? Are there challenging weaknesses you have turned into strengths? The more we struggle at something, the more it can point us in the direction of our purpose. You may receive joy by teaching others, which can come through this process.

Our Values and Principles

We discovered our values that we live by. We can use our values as a guideline in decision-making to be authentic to ourselves and to our purpose. Our purpose is usually weaved through the values we live by. These values create meaning for our purpose. When we are living through our values it aligns with our purpose. After you wrote your own principles, what lessons defined them? What were the key experiences that shape your principles? The more you learn from them, the more they can become a roadmap to help you level up as you live your life.

When we are in a state of authenticity, this is where our purpose shines through. This is where we start to weave it throughout our life. Both values and principles play a part in understanding our purpose at a deeper level. My values guide my decisions so I can show up for my purpose to serve others.

What's your greatest insight when it comes to your purpose? Are there principles you can create to help embody your purpose and live more authentically? These are all questions to help you understand yourself at a deeper level. To gain more clarity on your purpose and to live it each day.

Ikigai Model

The ikigai model allowed you to layer your understanding of your purpose through the overlapping core pillars. Did you find any of these sections correlated with areas piquing your interest? Did any unexpected insights emerge when you completed the ikigai model? Sometimes the overlapping sections reveal new opportunities. They can also help to reinforce what truly aligns with your purpose. Did you see new areas where you can apply your purpose in the world?

How did you find using AI to help generate ideas? Did you gain greater insights into the cross sections of passion, mission, vocation, and profession? For profession, were there jobs that piqued your interest? Were there jobs AI discovered that surprised you? Making you want to learn more?

Notice the patterns emerging from the ikigai model. Where did you have any epiphanies? Did you find gaps in an industry your skillset could fulfill? Your fresh perspective can translate those skills into something completely new. Are there new industries emerging in the markets? The ikigai model can open us up to new possibilities and perspectives. This can shift how we act and the direction we want to move in.

As you review the model, I want you to take a few minutes to close your eyes. Take some deep breaths and focus on your heart. Set an intention to identify your purpose. I want you to raise your vibrations by thinking of something joyful. I want you to feel this emotion throughout your entire body. Smile and be curious about what new information you will receive and new perspectives you will gain. Feel the excitement of new opportunities for your purpose to emerge. When you open your eyes, see what areas of your responses you are drawn to. Are there certain responses catching your attention? Take note and add these responses to your model.

Challenges

As you think back to your challenges you have overcome, what did you learn? What insights and wisdom did you gain? Did the experience change your priorities? Did it bring into focus what is important in your life? How did you overcome the challenge?

The struggles you review don't all have to be the most painful experiences. Sometimes even overcoming small obstacles with mind shifts are powerful lessons. It is the insights we gain that become invaluable. Which ones stand out to you the most? What lesson did you learn from the experience? Don't discount any challenges big or small.

When you review these challenges, also consider the strengths you gained and the weaknesses you were able to shed. Which versions of yourself were transmuted? What parts of yourself did you let go of and what new version of yourself emerged? One with more confidence? More understanding? Compassion? Perspective? Understand the transformation you made through the experience and take note of how it has shaped your purpose.

No Regrets

A powerful exercise we went through is building a relationship with death by writing your own obituary. This process helps you uncover hidden desires of what is still wanting to be created. It can be difficult to build a relationship with death, as most of us were taught to ignore it. When we stare into our own mortality it can help us live more intimately, giving us a window into a snapshot of our life. Letting us push past our comfort zone into where we truly want to live.

What did you learn from this exercise? What came up for you when you wrote your obituary? Did you see your purpose come through based on what you still want to do? Be compassionate while reflecting on this exercise. We tend to feel we need to be further along, comparing our chapter to others thinking we are far behind. You may still have many things you wish to accomplish in this lifetime. Prioritize them from the most important and what you are ready to commit to in taking steps to start.

Did you see key themes come from writing your obituary? Did a pattern emerge with the other exercises, creating more transparency around your purpose? Was there one thing in your obituary that stood out the most? Are you starting to see where your purpose is shining through? Reflect on these questions to gain better insights and how your purpose ties in.

Using Your Intuition to Connect with Purpose

Intuition is an amazing way to gain clarity. I know a lot of people who don't trust their intuition. They tend to rely mostly on logic, but this only gives us one element to work with. Relying solely on logic only considers the information in this moment.

When we use our intuition to guide us, we gain a vast array of knowledge we can tap into beyond space and time. It is a connection to something higher than us, giving us infinite wisdom beyond our current situation to make more informed decisions aligned with our higher calling.

Most people use their intuition without even knowing it. Have you ever thought about someone and then they text you? That's intuition. You may have had a flash of insight. Those moments that come when certain information clicks with a spark. We may start to see how seemingly unrelated events are linked. Almost like breadcrumbs for us to follow. This is what we call synchronicity because it confirms you are following your path.

Our intuition gets stronger when we have the courage to follow it. This starts to build "trust" within us. When you have that inspirational idea, you think, "I should do that!", but then your bossy mind will come in and start swinging its weight around. It will tell you all the reasons why you shouldn't do it.

You start rethinking this new inspiration by talking yourself out of it. "No, I couldn't do that. That would never work. What would people think?" We start backing out before we even begin. When this happens, start writing down baby steps for you to start taking action. You can also double-check with yourself. Perhaps there are more steps you didn't catch the first time.

It is key to understand that our intuition comes through our senses. This is why most people don't realize they are using it. The main ways we can connect with our intuition are through hearing, seeing, knowing, and feeling. There are others but these are the main ones we will focus on.

When we hear our intuition, it's called clairaudience. This doesn't mean you have to "hear voices". It can be the same voice as your internal dialogue. Chances are it is a quieter voice. Your intuition will be supportive, coming from a place of love. Your mind comes from a place of fear trying to keep you safe. This is a good way to start discerning the difference.

When you can see your intuition, it's called clairvoyance. Most people think only psychics have this ability. This is not true. An inspirational idea can come into your mind, and you see yourself taking action. You can use your imagination to tap into your intuition and visualizations.

Your intuition can come through by knowing, which is called claircognizance. Sometimes we know something at our core without being told. You know something to be true. You can feel it in your core. This intuition can be incredibly strong when it comes through.

Clairsentience is all about feeling. Your intuition can come through emotions and physical feelings in the body. This one is probably the most common. You have heard people talk about a "gut reaction." This is through feeling it in our body. When something is resonating with your intuition it can come through as a shiver down the spine. It could be a sensation. You may find it easy to connect with others' emotions. These are all ways our intuition can come through to give us wisdom.

When our intuition comes through multiple senses, this makes it stronger. Paying attention to the body and being present is key to working with our intuition. Reflect on these different ways your intuition comes through for you. Which one is the strongest? Focusing on the strongest sense first helps to give you confidence to work with the other senses.

Heart Connection

Now you know how your intuition can come through. My clients have found this practice to be one of the easiest ways to tap into your intuition. When we are in tune with our hearts, we can easily hear and feel our intuition. Most of us find it difficult to hear our heart or to feel its wisdom. This is like any muscle and the more you are consistent with the practice, the easier it becomes.

When we start to have a deeper awareness of our heart centre, it can also allow us to feel in certain situations. It can help to point us in the right direction when we are making decisions.

I talked about my heart tugging when my friend spoke about his grandfather volunteering at a hospice. I could feel it through my body. Over the next couple of weeks, I kept getting these confirmations to start walking this path. I would hear people talking about hospice. It kept coming up in conversations without me saying a word. These were synchronicities confirming what I was feeling.

The heart connection technique gets easier the more you do it. You want to sit in a quiet room where you won't be disturbed. It can be as long or as short as you would like. Set your intention to connect with your heart. Start by taking deep breaths and sink into your seat. Each exhale releases any expectations and starts to bring focus to your heart.

Each time you inhale visualize your heart expanding. See this synchronicity with your heart as you breathe. Feel how expansive your heart can be with each breath. You start to feel more in your body as you focus on your heart allowing your mind to take a break. Once you are in a cohesive rhythm with your heart, ask your question out loud. Wait and listen to hear a response from your heart.

Unlike our mind that can be noisy and bossy, our heart is usually softer. It has a quieter voice. At first it can be hard to discern between the two. Your heart comes from a place of love and compassion. The message will be supportive. Don't be frustrated if you don't hear anything at first. Use all your senses to see if messages come through hearing, seeing, knowing, or feeling. Write down your insights.

I have also found other ways to confirm your intuition. When I follow my intuition, I get this tingling sensation I call shimmers down my spine. Different from shivers, this feeling is almost like supportive vibrations down my spine. This is a confirmation for me to follow my intuition. Your intuition might come through differently. This is why it is important for you to keep practicing. It is how you start to understand how your body responds to your intuition. It is almost like learning a different language through our senses. Starting with our heart can be a gateway for the intuition to start flowing through. Our intuition can help us gain clarity on our purpose.

When we are present, it is easier to connect with our intuition. It sounds simple to be present but can be incredibly challenging. Our minds are very good at keeping us busy. It takes consistent action to stay present. We need to be curious and open to new experiences on our path. When we allow ourselves to be in a state of wonder and curiosity, we become immersed in our surroundings. We tend to notice things we wouldn't normally notice. We can be in a place of expansiveness.

Nature can help us stay in the present moment. You may find when you are walking or hiking your mind feels lighter. We can gain new insights we didn't even know existed. We can be more open to new ways of thinking. Movement helps us to be in the body instead of the mind. This is why being in nature is a great way to start harnessing your intuition. When we are curious, we are open.

Before you go out, set the intention you want to connect with your intuition. Ask to connect your greater insights into your purpose. Ask for this wisdom to come through your senses. Don't overthink it and leave the rest to your higher self. Know you have this innate wisdom inside of you that is waiting to be heard, felt, or seen. Allow for any insights to come through. Keep a small notepad to write down anything that comes to you.

Our intuition can help us gain a greater understanding of our purpose. When we need clarification, our hearts can point us in the right direction. The more you trust your intuition, the stronger it becomes. It can be a guiding light as you go through this journey. It can help you see bigger themes and patterns from the previous exercises. It can also help you weave a connection on how you want to start living your purpose. Be open to all possibilities.

Exercise: Clarity on Your Purpose

After reviewing all the exercises, start to create a list of insights you have gained.

1. What did you learn about yourself and your purpose?
2. What lights you up?
3. What are the key themes around your purpose?
4. Go out into nature and see what insights come to you about your purpose.
5. What inspirational moments have you had about your purpose?
6. What insights did you gain from doing the heart connection technique?
7. How did you find tapping into your intuition to gain more clarity around your purpose?
8. Is there something you want to create? A new business, a new job opportunity, volunteering, or hobbies that will help to fulfill your purpose?

What's Next...

In the next chapter we are going to explore the resistance you may go through when making changes in your life. When we want to do something different and carve out a new path, we can have resistance. There may be stories we tell ourselves that make us doubt our path. We are going to explore those aspects of ourselves, rewriting our stories so we can move forward with confidence.

Chapter 10

The Stories We Tell

By now you should have a pretty good idea of your purpose. If you haven't gone through all the exercises yet, I would invite you to go back to do them first. The insights they uncover are gold when it comes to self-discovery. You may just have an idea of how you want to live your purpose. That is okay if it's not concrete. This is better because it allows you to be open to the possibilities of how it will come into play. When we try to orchestrate the future, we can miss out on even bigger possibilities. Think of this process as co-creating with the universe. Each step you take toward your purpose unveils a new path beneath your feet. Trust the process.

There may have been a spark nudging you a certain way. If your purpose hasn't come through yet, don't despair. We are going to address the stories we may be telling ourselves that can block us from finding our purpose or moving forward toward it.

The stories I am referring to are the ones we tell ourselves to keep us small. These are the stories that suppress our capabilities. The stories starting with, "Yeah, that would be amazing to start living my purpose but…" When we immediately barricade our thinking with "but," it stifles your options. Think of it as an energetic barrier you are implementing within the language you choose. Our words do create magic.

If you don't think you can live your purpose, then you won't. It saddens me when I speak to people who feel like they are trapped because of the stories they tell themselves. It can range from, "I'm too close to retirement. I only have ten more years and then I can do what I really want" to "I have kids, a mortgage, I have bills" and "It would be great to start living my purpose and having a career that fulfills me but..." This is not to berate you if these are the thoughts swirling in your mind. It is an invitation to question them. To recognize them and start to unravel them.

These phrases limit our capabilities, and they also limit the lens we are looking through. They elicit fear around living our purpose and our truth. We create barriers to our own happiness when we allow our mind to tell us stories that are simply not true. A story that we must stay in the golden handcuff job because it pays the bills even though we are miserable. It is the story we say to ourselves that we cannot have financial security AND live our purpose.

One of my favourite books is *The Four Agreements* by Don Miguel Ruiz. He is a Toltec shaman who elaborates on the stories we tell ourselves. These are agreements we make. They become so powerful, we call them truths. A lot of the agreements we cling to hold us back. The worst part is most of them are untrue. Yet somewhere along the way our negative experience taints our self-worth, and we believe it. These stories create disharmony in our life. They try to keep us safe in a world with no guarantees.

Sadly, most of us are on autopilot and don't see the stories. We don't hear them in our minds or in the words we speak. Most of the time we don't even notice how we reinforce them. The fear our mind creates is one of the biggest reasons we don't take bigger leaps. We allow our mind to keep us small and most of the time we don't even realize we do it.

While fear is essential to our survival, recognizing when it holds us back is imperative. It is crucial not only to push outside our comfort zone but to release fear. Suzy Kassem sums it up perfectly, "Fear kills more dreams than failure ever could."

We have become very good at telling ourselves untrue stories and making them our truth. It is so subtle we may not even realize we have made them in the first place. The initial step is understanding how these stories block us in what we really want to achieve in our life. It is a hard truth to look in the mirror and see these narratives.

For most of my career I wanted nothing more than to climb the corporate ladder. I took personality and psychological tests in university and at work. I consistently got results aligning with entrepreneurship. My professors would tell me my personality was best suited to starting my own business. I remember scoffing at such an idea.

I would push it from my mind. Instead, I continued a path I would later realize came from a place of fear. I always worked for the largest and most established companies in their industry. This was my illusion of safety. In truth I was afraid. I was afraid to be on my own. No big organization to lead me. The irony is my personality is not one that was destined for corporate life. I could navigate it well enough throughout my career but again the emptiness grew. I yearned to do something different but was unaware of how to access this place inside myself. To truly allow myself to dream.

I stamped out the "What if's...". What if I take that leap of faith? What if I knew I couldn't fail? I could believe in myself to persevere. Sadly, the journey would take decades to uncover what I knew in my heart to be true. We tend not to pursue our dreams. Not because we can't accomplish the goal but because we are more afraid of failing. We fear others will see us fail and that would mean we are failures. We put the onus back on ourselves. Especially when we have a family we are supporting.

The stakes become high and in a lot of cases, too high for people to even try. To see what they have and to give themselves space to fail. There is this little voice in our head telling us we are not good enough, we are not strong enough, smart enough. It gets buried in our subconscious mind because it is uncomfortable facing our own fears. This is why we are going to explore these inner demons we keep locked inside. Most of the time we haven't built self-awareness to see how these little thoughts keep us small.

You may have had this revelation realizing there is a different path for you. You may have gone through all of the exercises and think to yourself, "This is what I really want to do!" You may feel a rush of energy thinking about following your purpose. Only for your mind to put the brakes on with a list of reasons why you can't pursue it.

Most of these thoughts usually come up around money. The financial burden of following our purpose usually creates golden handcuffs. We settle for our current position because it is familiar and safe. The illusion of security can be alluring. We are staying at a job we hate. A role we feel underappreciates and underutilizes our skillset. We feel small in the role. Only to wish for something different. A role with more meaning and fulfillment. A purpose to drive us forward.

We scoff at the idea that we deserve more. We can accomplish so much more if we pursue something completely different. I have seen people give up the golden handcuffs because they couldn't do it anymore. It was their turn to jump ship and find their own oasis in the distance. They knew there was something more for them.

The words and thoughts we think and say create our reality. Whether you believe this or not, language is powerful magic. Most of us don't pay attention to these words. When we try to justify something or explain away our actions, there are doubts lying beneath.

When I started my business and began making a real go of it, the question I dreaded the most was, "So what are you doing for work now?" Instead of saying, "I am a business owner, I am a leadership coach, I am speaker," I would try to explain away what I was doing. You could feel the discomfort in my demeanor because I felt like an imposter. Like I had already failed before I even began. I didn't have confidence in myself.

These were my own self-doubts lurking below the surface coming out in awkward ways. I didn't feel comfortable in my own skin because I wore so much armour for many years. Shifting how people saw me in the corporate world started to unravel my own self-limiting beliefs.

When we come up against our own fears, doubt can cloud the path. It can start to veer us off course into safer territory. A space where our mind feels safe. It is trying to help us from a survival perspective. These doubts are normal and will come up. The first step is to be aware of them and understand where they come from. Self-reflection is incredibly powerful and yet most of us spend a lot of time trying to avoid it.

Why? Because it is uncomfortable. It is uncomfortable to see ourselves exactly as we are without distancing from our faults. Facing the goals we missed and the failures we endured. Yet this step is necessary. It is necessary for us to grow and learn from our mistakes. To see these failures as stepping stones to our goals.

Understanding this dance with our mind is crucial. It helps us cultivate compassion when we start to procrastinate. When we start putting off our own dreams and living our purpose. This will happen. Knowing how to pivot, how to overcome these obstacles is invaluable. When we keep going, we see what is actually getting in the way. We pull apart the stories we are telling ourselves at a deeper level. Somewhere along the line we created an agreement calling it our truths.

We first reflect on where we are holding ourselves back. Where are we hesitating to dive in and to create momentum in our life? Where are we stalling and what is causing this reaction? Once we self-reflect on where we are afraid to be seen, where we are doing a disservice to ourselves by staying in the shadows, we then start to see the agreements we made. This can take time to unravel but first look at the words you are using. What are the excuses you are giving yourself? What is your mind telling you? Is this another agreement you made that is not true?

What evidence are you basing this agreement on? Most often it comes from a time when we were younger. We were told something and latched onto it as truth. We hold onto that moment and then it solidifies as an agreement.

I had mentioned that when I was younger, I was writing a story. I shared it with someone, and they laughed at it. They didn't even critique it, but I held onto that moment, creating an agreement that I couldn't write. I was too insecure to see it for what it was. Absolutely nothing. I took it as ridicule and stopped writing the story. I completely shut down.

Later in life when I was in high school, I wrote an essay about my parents' divorce, delving into this one moment I had as a child. Instead of giving me constructive criticism, the teacher ridiculed me in front of the entire classroom. It was the first time I had been vulnerable in my writing, sharing something that personal with anyone. He ridiculed me in the most humiliating way. The worst part is that he was my favourite teacher, which made the betrayal even deeper. It made me shut down further within my words and my voice.

Once we make this agreement on a subconscious level, it ripples through our actions. We seek out the smallest confirmation to support our agreement. We will disproportionately look at evidence reinforcing the agreement. This also feeds into cognitive bias. This is when we only look for evidence supporting our choice and rejecting evidence to the contrary. We look to validate these agreements wherever we see them. It normalizes the dissonance we have created within ourselves.

Our language can play an important part in understanding these agreements we made. When we are aware of our words, we can start to see patterns emerge. Reflect when you overexplain decisions, downplaying achievements or criticizing yourself with your words. Become the observer without judgement, replacing it with curiosity. When you do notice yourself dimming your light through actions and words, ask, "Where is this coming up for me?" "Is there a past experience being triggered within me?" If so, what is the underlying message you took away from the experience?

The first step in this journey always comes from self-awareness. Autopilot has become our default and has accelerated in the digital age. When we make this first initial step, we can start to see things more clearly. The next step is to see ourselves exactly as we are. Not with disdain or negative talk but with a true understanding of how we are. We can't start to make transformational shifts until this happens. This can be difficult and uncomfortable but necessary for us to grow. It can take a lot of courage not to beat ourselves down or create dissonance within us. The weaknesses, the self-talk, the battles we lost, the failures we place on our self-worth, we first must recognize these areas before we can start to shift our mindset until we can truly love ourselves unconditionally.

To love ourselves unconditionally doesn't mean we don't take accountability. It means we are embracing all aspects of ourselves. Even the parts we try to hide from. This is why finding the silver lining to our weaknesses can be such a powerful practice. We are no longer resisting but aligning. We must first embrace before we can transform.

When we are unaware of the power of our words it starts to bind us. When we constantly tell ourselves, "I can't do that," we are blocking it before we even begin. Our words create our reality. Our reality is based on a perception, and you get to choose the lens. If we constantly tell ourselves we can't do something, we won't succeed. These thoughts will find ways to prove we are right. Even when it is not the truth. When we block ourselves through words, it is all we see. We will only see the challenges in front of us.

The opposite is also true. When our words support us, they expand our perspective. We still face challenges, but we can create opportunities through adversity. You can see new ways of doing things, you can be more innovative and creative.

When we start this awareness process, we can start to change the narrative we are telling ourselves. We are now in the driver's seat of our awareness. To become fearless in our endeavour to create harmony within ourselves. This transformation does not happen overnight. It is a constant dance to be present and in harmony with our life. This is how we start to shed these negative and toxic patterns. It leads us to create new pathways, leading us to success by cheering us on.

These are the layers we pull back from our veil in order to start seeing the bigger picture. We can start to see ourselves exactly as we are. It can be uncomfortable but necessary to create the life you truly want and to believe in yourself. We can't look externally for our validation and our happiness. This is an inward journey. To support your new path and overcome any challenge.

Fear of Failure

A lot of people don't pursue their dreams or their purpose because there is a deep-seated notion that we will fail. In a society that covets perfectionism, no wonder there is a fear of failure. There is no path we take in life where failure is not on the table. It is a part of life, and it is how we learn from our mistakes in order to grow.

Yet we tend to wear success and failure as a badge of honour, placing our self-worth on both our triumphs and flops. One of the biggest fears is around, "What will people think?" We don't think other people's opinions matter until we do a deep dive within ourselves. Then watch it show up. You can usually tell when we overanalyze conversations, afraid we might be seen in the wrong light.

At the end of the day, ask yourself, "Who fucking cares?" In the grand scheme of things, what does this really say about yourself? You swung and you missed. You recalibrate and you learn. This is your story. No one else's. This is your life, and the best part of our life is we get to tell it. Not to manage everyone's expectations of us.

The truth is we cannot control what others think or do. However, we do have a choice in how it will affect us. We have a choice in how we react and become aware of what is going on inside our mind. We can choose new supportive agreements to nurture ourselves. We have the choice to be compassionate and love ourselves no matter what.

One of the biggest challenges I have experienced in my career is imposter syndrome. I have experienced this throughout my career. When we are not careful it can diminish our confidence without us even realizing it. Imposter syndrome is when we don't attribute our success to our abilities, instead believing our success is due to external factors. Most of the time it plays out when we don't feel worthy in our role. You are afraid people will find out that you are not as smart as people think. You don't believe in your own capabilities despite all your accomplishments to the contrary.

A staggering 70 percent of people will experience imposter syndrome at some point in their life[22]. Ironically, it mostly affects high achievers. They are usually harder on themselves and tend to be perfectionists. Imposter syndrome can rear its ugly head when we pursue something new. Changing careers, going after our dreams, and committing ourselves to pursue our purpose. It can contribute to us putting off our own happiness or rebuffing our ability to even try.

I believe imposter syndrome is highly correlated with our self-worth. When we don't value who we are as a person, we distance ourselves from our own achievements. We downplay our success and feel there is an unfair advantage that was given to us. While

---

[22] Daniel Goleman, "Therapists Find Many Achievers Feel They're Fakes," *The New York Times*, Sept. 11, 1984, https://www.nytimes.com/1984/09/11/science/therapists-find-many-achievers-feel-they-re-fakes.html.

this can be the case, cultivating our self-worth is incredibly important to push outside our comfort zone.

I interviewed Rebecca Llewellyn (www.yourdivineroots.com), a shamanic and breathwork practitioner owner of Divine Roots. She is a friend and mentor who helped me find my voice and purpose. She also started in the corporate world for a decade until she branched out helping others heal and walking with them on their path. She also experienced imposter syndrome, feeling she needed more and more certifications to feel ready. While time is required to step into our wisdom and purpose, we also need to unravel the stories keeping us from living it. "Every experience prepared me for the next one. It is a process over time spiraling upward and unwinding the stories of receiving, self-worth, and value."

Taking a new direction even when others can't see it is scary. It takes courage, and this is why self-worth is so important. It's important not only for your success but also to believe in yourself to be successful. A lot of us were not taught to love ourselves unconditionally. We were told to disdain weaknesses in others. We were taught to judge and fit in a perfect box. Yet our self-worth comes from the love we have within ourselves. To love ourselves exactly as we are.

These wounds inside us need to be addressed to be able to open ourselves up to unconditional love. Our love is considered conditional when we continue to deny the parts we don't like. We cannot truly heal until we embrace all aspects. This is something we don't need to wait for someone else to give to us. We have the power to give it to ourselves. This is a key concept to help overcome our fears and ways we block ourselves. Unravelling the stories we have told in our mind around not feeling we are good enough. To replace them with new and supportive ones. By still having the compassion to embrace these wounds.

When we can love ourselves unconditionally, we no longer seek approval from others. We don't need to seek validation. We already have it within us. This is what nourishes us to show up as our best. Even when we fall, we can pick ourselves back up and dust off without it becoming a stain on our self-worth. You are all the validation you will ever need. You are all the love you will ever need. No one dictates your worth except you.

It can be hard sometimes not to get stuck in our story. The challenges we've overcome and how we see those challenges shape our story. We can see ourselves as a victim or the hero of our narrative. We have the choice to shape our world. To create our own reality based on our thoughts and our actions. If we see only pain and struggle, we invite more into our life. We draw it closer to us. On the flipside when we see the growth and the challenges we have overcome, we can empower our story.

I was having a conversation late one night with my friend who has endured a lot in her life. She said, "We get to create our own narrative." I thought about how powerful that statement can be to set us free. It can be easy to slip into the victim mentality. To feel completely helpless and trapped by our circumstances. However, we can move through the pain, move through the challenge and come out on the other side. We can create an empowered narrative.

We are the ones who choose the direction of our life. The lens we pick to view the perspective of our circumstance. When we are in a victim mentality, we feel like life is being done to us. While life will throw us many curve balls and a lot of them will be unavoidable, we do get to choose how we meet them.

We can choose the mind shift of how we determine to meet these challenges. Will we hide under the covers and not face them, will we scream and blame others, or will we meet them head-on? Will we have the compassion to allow ourselves to make mistakes? To learn from them and move forward. To see the growth and expansion we can all have within ourselves.

Remember, your life has not been written yet. You get to choose each day. You are given the choice of how to live your purpose. You are the one who gets to be the hero in your story. No matter the life you have lived, you get to choose your own narrative. One of empowerment or one as a victim trapped in the pages.

Shifting our mindset is crucial to pursuing our purpose and leading a more engaged life. It doesn't come without work or courage, but it is understanding how your mind correlates to your purpose. Do you feel excitement, trepidation, or resistance with a hard no? What is your initial reaction when you think about pursuing your dreams? Pursuing your purpose within your career?

Introspection allows us to understand ourselves better and recognize when fear is blocking our path. It allows us to embrace the discomfort. To pull back the layers and move forward in alignment. There are endless opportunities to feed our purpose, if we have the courage to take action.

Exercise: Uncovering the Resistance

This exercise can be uncomfortable at first because we are becoming aware of our mind. No judgement or berating but full awareness of both the proverbial "good" and "bad". Set an intention in the morning to become more aware of the false stories you are telling yourself. This can be hard at first because you are jumping into full gear of your awareness. To create a habit of self-awareness, set an alarm once an hour. Check in with yourself and see what is coming up for you. Write down your thoughts. No judgement, but just witness your internal dialogue.

Part 1: Self-Awareness

- What are the thoughts you have been having?
- How often are your thoughts positive or negative?
- Write down these thoughts in a journal.

As you go through this exercise, try not to judge or change the narrative but become aware of it.

Part 2: Replacing Agreements

- Journal about the self-talk you caught throughout your day.
- What are the stories you are telling yourself?
- Reflect if there was an experience in your past that created this false story.
- What are new agreements you are going to make to replace these stories?

Be kind through this process because this will be an ongoing practice. We are peeling back the layers to the stories and replacing them with new ones. This is necessary to start changing our narrative.

What's Next...

The next chapter is more fun because we get to create a new vision. A vision of the future we are co-creating with the universe. We are going to start building this vision and learning how to embody it to align with your goals.

Chapter 11

Creating a Spark Through a Vision

Once we have established our purpose and worked through our resistance, the next step is to start building a vision. We can't set a course for where we want to go until we see it. Until we embody it and move along the path.

Working on this vision is important not only to see yourself succeeding, but also to build the confidence to get there. It can be daunting to see a vision so big we can't possibly see the path to victory. When we focus too much on how we are going to get there, we block the fun of not knowing. We try to manage how things will manifest. The truth is the journey is wilder than you can imagine. So don't limit how it comes to you. Just start with your North Star.

If you feel like there is still resistance, don't despair. Continue to peel back these layers. Revisit the old stories and revise. Resistance can be a helpful tool to know where to focus. To work through the stories and untruths no longer serving you.

When we create this vision, we want to clearly see the outcomes, even if they seem unrealistic at this point. When we start building this reality, we want to not only see it but feel it. Everything is energy. The vibrations we carry inside us will resonate with the outcomes we choose.

Emotions such as joy, love, and laughter have a higher vibration. They create expansive opportunities with the ability to see them and act. When we are in lower states of vibrations, it creates a narrow mindset limiting the doors we can open.

Think of this vision as the seeds we first need to plant. We need to be intentional with where we plant them, tending to our loving thoughts and nourishing our vision. The more positive vibrations we feed into our vision, the more sunlight it creates for expansion. Then with our actions we sustain the vision like refreshing water. The roots begin to take hold. When the vision is stable it can grow into something truly wonderful.

We need to feel this energy and the magic we create with our thoughts and intentions. We need to do this with intentional action. It can be hard not to go after the shiny objects. I did this for years. I was focusing my time on the bells and whistles instead of what will truly make an impact.

Visions are important to help us focus our time and our energy on where we want to go. We don't want to get stuck on the how. The universe will help us get there when we pay attention. When we see past the obstacles and look for the lessons hidden within. The opportunities along the hidden path.

We use our vision to focus on the future of our destiny. It can allow us to be more open to new ways of being, expanding our mind in the most amazing ways, but we must be in a high vibrational state. This will not always be the case, but we can start with our level of awareness. It is a balance of knowing where we are going but still being in the present moment.

When we are constantly in the future or the past, we unintentionally create blocks. The worry of the mistakes we made in the past and the worries of the future lower our vibrations. Focusing on our heart will allow us to be present. The state of our heart will allow us to expand and transform. It is no easy feat.

Manifestations are usually blocked in two ways. The first is focusing on scarcity. The fear of the future, the unknown, and usually money. Trust is hard to cultivate when we are in these vibrations. The second is focusing solely on making money. Financial abundance can flow when we are not holding on so tightly.

This intuitive message came through to me multiple times. It will stifle abundance if this is your sole intention. The gratitude we have each day for what we already have. The feeling of abundance within us. This can be one of the hardest things to validate. To see the accomplishment and success we already possess. To embrace within. When we recognize our accomplishments, it swells. We are the masters of our destiny not by what we give to the outside world but give to ourselves. The grace, the dignity, and the self-love to see it happen. This can be a monumental moment for all of us to feel success within us.

Since our thoughts are constantly trying to keep us safe, it will block these visions. It will try to cast doubt on your abilities. The stories can come back during these stages, the ones we addressed with resistance. This is a constant dance to align with your future state.

Merging your future self with your current self is key. You are essentially aligning the energy of your future self in the present. If you knew you couldn't fail, how would you feel right now? How would you act differently? The self-doubt would be non-existent. We would have empowerment even in the eye of a storm. Even in the darkness and confusion there would be an inner peace of knowing, of trust that it will work out. That the sun will rise again even if it has been years since the light has touched your face.

Faith is part of the equation, yet so many of us were taught to doubt. To be skeptical and discern. We were taught to judge. If it is too good to be true, then it probably is. A sad statement uttered so many times. All these doubts and fears block us from our vision.

Another aspect of the vision where blocks can show up is what we are envisioning. A lot of people focus on the financial aspect. The answer for them is more money. I want to be rich. I want to be financially wealthy. I don't want to work. The challenge with using money as a vision is not sustainable. Money is a vehicle, it's not the impact.

You want to focus on the impact. What do you want to do with the money? What is the intrinsic value? If your goal is to not work because you have enough money, then what are you doing? Why are you doing it? The money allows you to create, to inspire to make an impact. This is the focus of the vision and how it makes you feel. This goes back to your purpose and what fulfills you.

Money allows these things to happen, to help more people do more things, but it is not the main driver.

When it is your main driver, it is a trick keeping you on the marigold round. It usually stops us from going after our purpose in the first place. This is the illusion of money. The financial trap. We feel money will justify our self-worth, which it does not. You are constantly reaching for it but feel like it is always just out of reach. When this becomes the main driver, we create a cycle of chasing money to justify our internal worth. And around and around we go. Only we can give ourselves the love of self-worth. Since this is an internal journey, it starts with us. It starts with our own love and the vibrational aspects. Not the other way around.

Money is an energetic exchange instead of just physical money. When we are in scarcity mode, we try to hoard money, but this creates more scarcity, not abundance. The words we use when we speak to ourselves such as, "I never have enough money" create more scarcity and around and around we go.

More debt, more financial burdens. We only see the negative aspect of money because it is what we see inside ourselves. "I am not good enough. I don't deserve money." We only see it as external factors against us. This is an inside job shifting our mindset with money. We can create more momentum to build this inside ourselves. This is part of our vision when we start to clear these blockages, and these stories ultimately hold us back.

Vibration Resonance

We are all made of energy and connected to the world through energy. Our emotions and thoughts create a vibrational frequency resonating with our reality. Bringing a vision into reality is not easy. Yet most manifestation gurus make it sound so easy to bring our dreams toward us. Think happy thoughts and build a vision. However, there is more to it. There are other factors to consider. We have way more negative thoughts than positive ones. Building a vision for our future is only one step. It is important we become very clear on what the vision will entail.

We need to understand what specific details about the vision are most important to us. When we create this vision, we need to feel it in our heart. Not only in one moment but it needs to be a constant reminder throughout the day. We need to draw our future self into this reality. We need to start living as if we are already this person. We cannot "hope" this will happen.

When we are constantly worrying and have made up our mind it won't happen, guess what? It won't. It will always be out of reach because our mind is telling us we are not worthy of what we truly desire. We go back to our stories, and they can start to haunt us. When this happens, it will slow down the energetic alignment of your dreams and purpose.

Perhaps you want to switch careers in a different industry and within a different area. These are two hurdles put into the path. It will be harder, but not impossible. When we keep telling ourselves how difficult it is, we narrow the path with more obstacles. These hurdles are testing points. When you start to declare what you truly want to come into fruition, you will be tested. You will experience setbacks and obstacles. This is important to remember. Just because you declare something does not make it easy no matter what the gurus tell you.

I am telling you this not to scare you but to prepare you. Nothing worth doing was done because it was easy. Especially when it comes to breaking out of our own box. Doing something completely different and transforming our lives. It takes practice, experimenting, faith, and a whole lot of self-love. It takes dedication to yourself. It will bring up the things you fear the most because when we face them, we expand.

Your path might not align with everyone else. That is okay. Hell, it is better than okay! It means you are innovating. You are growing and expanding. One of the hardest things I had to do was stop looking at what everyone else was doing. It brings up fear and comparison within us. We start to think we are so far behind compared to everyone else. We beat ourselves up because we feel we are falling behind. It creates those fearful emotions that we are not doing the "right" things. It will throw you off your game chasing all the shiny objects.

This can be one of the biggest blockers when it comes to raising our vibrations to meet our vision. When we compare ourselves to other people it makes us feel less worthy. It makes us question whether we are going to make it. It can cause resentment and victimize us as we wonder why it has worked out for them and not us. This is a trap that we can fall into that will only create blockages and unhealthy mind patterns.

Start to walk a different path and release the mind with all the noise. You are following a path no one else has trekked because you are unique. You have something no one else has to offer. You are an original mess of experiences, successes, and pitfalls. You have a novel view that no one else can replicate because it is uniquely yours. Own it!

Own your experience and catch yourself comparing your life to someone else's. Notice it, become aware, and let it go, knowing in your heart your life is meant for another path forward. I am not saying that you shouldn't see how others have made it. Learning is one thing I hold dear more than anything else to expand and grow. Make sure you don't try to replicate someone else to the point you lose your authenticity. This is what makes you so special. Your experiences and your life journey.

When you are envisioning the future, I want you to focus on who you are. When you visualize yourself achieving all these amazing goals, how are you different? What are the thoughts on your mind? How has your confidence shifted? Do you look different? How have you grown and shifted to achieve everything you have wanted to manifest?

The reason you want to get clear on your future self is because this is the frequency you need to vibrate at. You need to focus your attention on knowing this is you. When you are already embodying your future self, you will draw the right people toward you. You can see the opportunities. You can know how to overcome obstacles because you have done it already in the future.

Shifting from hope to knowing can take some time. It is a habit that needs to be applied with discipline. We tend to come from a state of fear. Fear can creep up in the way we feel uncertain about situations. We try to provide a spin with optimism, yet we don't feel it in our bones. It's hard to trust ourselves and what we are truly capable of creating in our future.

Instead, we wish. We wish situations to change, to turn positive, but it is fear creeping in the background. Wishing still vibrates with underlying fear. When we are grounded in who we are there is trust. It creates confidence within us. We are in a state of co-creating with the universe. This is where magic happens. It starts with us getting out of our head. Not trying to fixate on how things will turn out, but trusting it will turn out for our highest potential.

Spending our time trying to control outcomes and control others comes from a place of fear. It is counterproductive and exerts an immense amount of energy. It creates frustration, burnout, and can also be incredibly triggering. When we surrender to the unknown, this is where we can truly trust. We can allow ourselves to unfold in a state of love and abundance. This is a balancing act, which can be incredibly difficult for people to grasp.

This is where using our intuition guides us on this journey of self-discovery. Our intuition is an innate state of knowing. It is a deeper wisdom within us. This is where knowing instead of hoping becomes so profound. Sadly, most of us were taught to follow our logical minds. Follow the logic and this will lead you where you need to go. I did this for many years, only following my mind. I did all the things I was "supposed" to do. Go to a good school, get my master's degree, go into business because "logically" it has the best options. Follow the crowd because logically it is the best route in life. Yet most of us end up on this marigold ride of feeling unfulfilled.

We are listening to everyone else instead of our own wisdom, our own intuition. Stop listening to the outside world telling you what you need to do. Start listening to the ancient wisdom you have always carried inside of you. It is energetically there, waiting to be unlocked by you. Waiting for you to start trusting your own instincts to know what you can do with your life.

If this resonates with you, you are already following your intuition. You are already looking at a different path for yourself. This is the first step, and it can be the scariest step to follow because it goes against the grain. Following something you weren't taught to use on a regular basis is uncomfortable. Especially when it contradicts our mind. It is a scary thought to go against logic.

When you start this path of self-discovery and follow your intuition, it will be uncomfortable. Those looking in may think you are crazy. What do you mean you are leaving a "good job"? What do you mean you are taking a leap of faith? It can be lonely knowing you are on the right path but only you see it. Just know this is completely normal. This will happen because when we start to break the cycles of the standard path, society starts to push back. It feels uncomfortable because you are not following the flock. However, when we use our intuition as a guidepost, this is your internal compass. It will help to strengthen your "knowing" and you will no longer be "hoping" or "wishing". You are slowly trusting your inner knowledge to create a pathway to a life you truly want to lead.

When I was younger, I would see people speaking on stage and captivating audiences. I would think to myself, "I wish I could do that. I wish I could teach people something amazing to help them. I wish I had that type of wisdom and knowledge to help others."

You do! We all do. We just haven't tapped into it. We haven't learned to lead from a place of knowing.

If we continue in the frequency of wishing, this is where it will stay. It cannot transform and manifest into the physical realm if we don't make a bigger impact with action. You have to act even in the smallest capacity to start making it a reality.

This feeling of abundance and this inner knowing cannot only be when you create the vision. This is an ongoing process we want to live throughout the day. In and out knowing you are going to be successful in your endeavor to start living your purpose.

It does take time to shift our habits, so we become aware of our thoughts, actions, and words. If we are resonating with lower vibrations and do not feel we are worthy, this will be a difficult path indeed. Trust me, starting out by releasing these stories at the beginning will help you immensely. If these stories keep popping back up, review the last chapter in more depth.

Set your intention for your vision and be clear about what you want to create in your life. The financial aspect should support the vision. What will the money allow you to do? Focus on the impact you will make with the monetary value. It is a tool to allow us to accomplish the things we want to do. Money has a frequency, this is why when we try to hold on so tightly, it can block. Think of the financial aspects as an exchange of energy. Reciprocity through impact can actually create more financial abundance in your life. This is a law of reciprocity. The more you give to others, the more you receive.

Future Self

You first want to set your intention for your vision. Next focus on what you want to achieve. You want to see yourself in the future having already achieved these goals. You want to feel the emotions of joy, success, gratitude, and appreciation. When we feel these emotions, our energy vibrates at a higher frequency. It starts to draw this reality toward us.

See yourself in the future achieving your goals. Draw them into this reality by embodying their qualities. The gaps between our present and future self allow us to focus on the growth. This version in the future will accelerate your goals by bridging the gap between the two.

This is why I asked the question about what is different when you see yourself in the future. You want to start getting incredibly specific on the qualities your future self has acquired. You want to start finding out where the gap is between your future self and your current self.

You are more likely to create more abundance following your future self to see how they got there. Seeing different opportunities coming your way and how you achieve them. What are the qualities you have yet to put into place? How has incorporating your purpose changed and transformed you?

Start to visualize not only your future self but the tasks you need to complete to become this person. Are they more confident? How can you embody this aspect of yourself? Remember, in the future you have already done it. This actually makes the experience less scary. You are the one completing and accomplishing everything in your path. This is another way for you to understand the power of the magic you have inside of you.

Remember, this is not some person who is randomly achieving your dreams. It is YOU, transforming your life to achieve them. To stop putting off what you in your heart know is important to you. Knowing the steps you create now are the ones that will help you to be the best version of yourself. You are not going to be in this state all the time. You are going to fail. You are going to question your path. That is okay, it is normal to go through this state of questioning.

It is part of how we continue to work through the mind constantly questioning everything. Your mind will try to make you second-guess your decision. Keep going anyway! When you are no longer on auto pilot you will start to hear and see everything. You will recognize how your mind keeps you small. The fears it instils with each little comment. You can see the patterns and how they fit in the bigger picture. You always have the choice to make a different decision.

You can use walking meditation to start embodying your vision for the future. This can be done anywhere when you are walking out in nature or down the street. You want to first get a clear image of your future self when you do this practice. I want you to see them so clearly in your mind. I want you to see how they walk. How they hold themselves. The thoughts they think about. The areas are grounded in their beliefs and ideas.

I want you to start using this as a way for you to walk like them. I want you to create each step that you are taking to walk into the future. You see this transition morphing into the person you were always meant to be. Walk with intention. Start to open your mind to their thoughts and actions. Notice how the mind is now a part of their conscious and waking state.

The more you can embody your future self into your every day, the faster you will accelerate. I was experimenting with this process and exercise as a gateway to embody my future self. It can also be fun and liberating. For example, when I was doing crunches as my future self, I was instantly able to do more reps, almost doubling what I could previously do. It is pretty miraculous when we start to embody our future self in the present moment. It opens the door to new possibilities without our mind creating roadblocks with self-limiting beliefs.

When I tried this with yoga it was such a transformational moment because yoga allows you to be present. Embodying my future self allowed me to be more connected to the land. I found that I could reach out with my energy and feel this surge throughout my body. I was more playful and less rigid. I was more confident and grateful about exactly where I was in life. It created a deep sense of knowing in myself.

When you embody your future self in the present moment, it releases self-limiting beliefs, allowing you to release the fears. Allowing for expansive ways of thinking because in the future you have already done it. The fear of failing starts to melt away. You accelerate your growth because you are closing the gap between now and in the future. When you tap into this part of yourself, you are tapping into the wisdom already available to you. This allows you to go faster and collapse time frames.

You are getting a sneak preview and drawing it toward you now. This can be incredibly useful for you to start creating and taking this as part of your own actions. How can you use this information to your advantage and put it into action now? How can you close this gap when you are walking with the intention of your future self?

You want to embody your future self but still want to be grounded in the present moment. Try not to overthink. Set the intention before you begin the activity. You are going to embody this future self who has achieved your dreams. They have manifested this beautiful reality, which you are now enjoying. This is your future, so you want stay present while projecting this frequency in the world.

When you are tapping into this future version of yourself you will have this gratitude. It will help to elevate your vibration to resonate with this reality. Gratitude is an important factor when we talk about manifesting and creating our reality. When we want to draw new realities toward us, gratitude will help us to take aligned action. We are coming into this state of abundance when we focus on gratitude. It allows us to get out of our mind of comparison.

When we are aware enough to start tracking these thoughts, we can start to pull ourselves out. We can recognize when our mind is going down a toxic spiral. We can ground back into gratitude. This helps us refocus and feel the abundance we already have. The love and support in our life. Even if you are in a place where you find gratitude to be difficult. Go for a walk in nature and be grateful for all the trees that are there to support you. The connection and the air that is purified by the forest. Connect with nature and breathe in the gratitude that they are there for us. This can help us to get out of our head. Realize how connected we are to everything all around us.

Your own unique journey has been designed to lead you to your destiny. This masterpiece you create with your words as the brush, your thoughts the paint, and your vision as the outline. The inspiration to create lasting change in your life. You are on this beautiful path to discovery, but it doesn't mean that it is easy.

You must consciously put up your hand and say, "There is a better way I can live my life that is aligned with my purpose." You are taking the unbeaten path to get there. You don't need the whole roadmap at this point. Only the conviction to endure the hardships. Knowing in yourself that you can achieve anything you set your mind to. Clarity comes when we have the conviction to move forward even with little steps.

Use key times to visualize your future self and make it a habit. Visualize your future self in the morning when you first wake up. Feel the emotions and vibrations to help create this mind shift as your morning just begins. We tend to focus on what we must do that day. You may not even be a morning person, and that is okay too. We can still create habits to support us in making this shift. It is small but powerful. The more you do this practice in the morning, the more resilience it builds. You will be able to see those opportunities over the hardships that come your way.

Another useful time is before bed. Visualize your future self and the vision you have created. This will help you to be in a confident state of your life. This time of day is also important because you'll stay in higher vibrations as you fall asleep. When we are stepping into this vision, it will help stop your mind from racing. It will help mitigate the worries we have when sleeping.

Lastly, create a habit to check in with yourself throughout the day. See yourself accomplishing the goals you have set out in front of you. This can be one of the hardest tasks because we may not feel confident. You may wonder if this is the right path or if perhaps your massive leap in a different direction will be worth it. See that vision throughout the day to bring you back to yourself, to your knowing, and faith that you will be successful.

When we first start this process, it can be hard to remember throughout the day. You are still trying to create supportive habits. Using timers to remind you to come back to this vision. Allow yourself to feel the gratitude about how far you've come. The stepping stones that have brought you to this moment, even if you feel this is the beginning part of your journey. Your journey has been lifelong. All the skills, the experiences and life lessons have led you to this moment. Keep going! Celebrate those successes. Celebrate that you have set this intention to create a new path. To realize you were meant for something different.

Creating a vision is different than daydreaming. Dreaming about how our life can be different can help to start the vision. Yet this is not where we want to stay. You are embodying this person in the present moment. Dreaming can create a separateness from us. We see all the things we want but don't feel like we deserve it. This will always keep it out of reach because it is a state of "wishing" or "hoping" instead of "knowing". Remember the difference.

You are worthy of your success and accomplishments, so bring this higher vibration into this moment.

Keep the vision alive through the rollercoaster of life. Your future self can help you to make different decisions and bold choices than your current self. When you are faced with a difficult decision, or you are not sure what to do next, tap into your future self.

Visualize them in front of you. Ask for their advice and start to embody them within your daily tasks. You have so much untapped wisdom inside of you. This is a way to accelerate and unlock it now. "Is that even possible?" In the words of Han Solo, "I never ask that question until after I've done it."

When we are visualizing our future self and our new path, it can be hard not to set limitations. To doubt what is possible and play small. Our mind may look at our future self and scoff at the thought of a reality where this is possible. Be aware when your mind starts to micromanage your vision. Your mind might ask questions like, "How could this be possible?" You may start trying to think of all the steps necessary to create this reality. You may become dejected and not understand how it could be possible. This type of thinking will block you before you even begin.

This is not to say we don't take action. This is an incredibly important part of bringing our new future into our reality. The difference is we will take intentional action. You will learn more about this in the next chapter. As part of the vision, just know you don't need to have every step planned out. We have to be open to adaptation and flowing with our vision.

When we are open to new opportunities in our life, it creates more possibilities. To do this we have to surrender to our vision. Not controlling the journey but allowing it to unfold when we are open and in expansive states. This is what higher vibrations create, the ability to see things from a higher perspective. We can identify new opportunities and overcome our challenges. We start co-creating with the universe instead of trying to micromanage our way through it with only the mind to guide us.

Don't set limitations on yourself through your mind about what is possible and what is not. You are an infinite being and anything is possible, but only if you allow it to be so. Start creating the magic I know you have inside of yourself. Know it is slowly coming toward you. You are drawing it into your life with your vibrations and actions. You will create an amazing adventure, and it is all here for you. Believe in yourself to make it happen.

Exercise: Building Your Vision

In this exercise we are going to start building that vision of your future self. We are going to get incredibly clear on all the aspects of this new version of you. I want you to set aside ten minutes of your time. Find a place in your home or in nature where you won't be interrupted to complete this meditation. You can download the meditation as part of your free gift[23].

Start taking some deep breaths and start to see yourself in the future. They have accomplished the goal you are working on. I want you to paint a picture in your mind that you can see so clearly. I want you to feel the emotions of having succeeded.

Start to take notice of the following:

- What looks different in them?
- Do they walk differently? Is their posture different?
- What are you doing in the future?
- Feel into their emotions and energy of succeeding in completing your dreams.

Questions to ask your future self:

- How is their thought process different now?
- How do they deal with self-doubt in the future?
- What can you do differently to start embodying them on a regular basis?
- What is the most important thing you need to know in this moment?

---

[23] www.fearlesslotus.com/freegift

What's Next...

Congratulations on making it this far! You now should have a pretty good idea of what lights you up as part of your purpose. You have delved into the stories. Lastly, you have created a vision for how you want your life to transform. How you want your purpose to be a part of your life. In the last chapter we focus on how you can create "intentional" action to align with your new path forward.

Chapter 12

Your North Star

Moving forward toward your North Star is crucial for us to start creating the life we want. We now are going to start incorporating our purpose within our life. This is not about trying to do everything at once or even making massive shifts. This can move quickly or slowly depending on your energy and how you work. The important thing to remember is being intentional with your action. This will help to create alignment on your path and mitigate burnout.

This is where we start to build out a plan for you to create those stepping stones to lasting change. Whether this is through finding a new role aligned with your purpose, starting a new chapter in retirement, or looking to spend more of your free time dedicated to living your purpose. You will want to be intentional about where you want to go.

Remember the vision we built and the exercises within the vision to keep you on track toward your goal ahead. This can be an exciting and scary time because you are trekking a new path. You may still have some resistance. That is okay and completely understandable. There will be a back and forth when we start something new in our lives. We have hesitation and doubts. This is where you want to refer to chapter 10 to help you release them.

This is the chapter where we will build out a plan for you to get to your destiny. The best piece of advice I can give you is to keep moving. The reason I want to point this out to you is because I dragged my feet for years. I would have been way further ahead if I had jumped in with both feet. If I had the courage to go all-in at the beginning. However, I had a lot of self-doubt to release. I needed to unravel my stories and create the courage to be seen. To be in my own element.

Depending on your own experiences, personality, and style, this will be different for you. The point is that you are here now. You made it this far and you are still going. You are creating a new path forward and moving toward your own destiny.

Set the intention to reach your North Star, releasing all the noise in your mind telling you it is too far away. Asking you questions like, "How am I supposed to get there?" Let it go. You don't need to know how you are going to get there. This is worth repeating because this can be a big hurdle to overcome. You DO NOT need to know how you are going to get there.

Think about some amazing experiences you've had over the years. Think about times when you met the right person at the right point. How a job fell into your lap or a referral leading to a new opportunity aligned perfectly. I have heard people's success stories and almost all of them include comments like, "I was at the right place at the right time. Everything aligned perfectly." It didn't mean they didn't have to put in the work. They acted, but almost like magic a new path opened up they didn't expect.

Most of us have experienced this alignment showing us a new path. Someone mentions something sparking a new idea, a new way of being, or an innovation. This is how life operates. When we stop blocking ourselves and trying to figure out "how" it is going to happen, we can start experiencing the way things are meant to happen. You don't have to figure out every step of the way. It not only dulls the experience of living but also blocks unique ways your dreams can unfold. When we start to see only one path to success, it can feel daunting. It also puts a lot of pressure on you to try to make it happen a certain way. It creates unnecessary resistance in your life. We are trying to orchestrate our manifestations and trust me, that creates more hardships along the way.

When we try to orchestrate how things are going to happen it can block us. We feel that our logical mind must figure it out before it happens. Unfortunately, we are not great at predicting the future or how we are going to get there. So why would you waste your time trying to do it? It doesn't mean you don't have a plan, but be open to how things will fall into place.

This is where we want to be open to all ways and opportunities. I will give you an example of how I tried to orchestrate a manifestation and ended up blocking it for a year. When we made the decision to buy a house a few years back, the market was the worst. It was after the pandemic and housing prices skyrocketed. Bidding wars were insane and everyone wanted to leave the city. They wanted more space just like us. Our realtor and friend, Megan tried to convince us to move farther out of the city. We were looking at some of the cities closer by because we wanted to commute to Toronto.

She kept trying to nudge us closer to Hamilton. We did not want to move to Hamilton. We didn't know the city that well and it was a lot farther than where we wanted to be. So we kept saying no and looked at other towns. This went on for almost a year. I became so tired of looking at houses and feeling like nothing was working out. I was so exhausted trying to make these other places work out, I finally threw up my hands and said, "Fine Universe, you choose for me. Where am I supposed to be?"

I decided to surrender. I finally stopped trying to "orchestrate" how these opportunities were going to come toward me. Instead, I finally opened up all the doors to whatever was meant for me. I released control. I asked Megan, "Where should we be?" I finally was starting to trust the process where I didn't get to control how I got there but I still had the vision of where I was going. I didn't try to block any places because I knew in my heart we would end up where we were meant to be.

A friend of mine was hosting a sound bath focusing on connecting with your guides. I went into this deep meditation and asked my guides to show me my house. I was instantly transported to an attic. It looked like it was a walk-up with matching windows on either side. The floors were hardwood, and the ceiling painted white. I saw it as my sanctuary to do rituals, meditation, and perhaps yoga. It gave me peace knowing our home was still out there.

As I continued our search for our home, I kept looking for the attic. Within a week there was a house we put a bid on, and we were the highest offer. Megan called me to say she had some awkward news. They went with a lower bid but had a bigger down payment cheque. She said it was something she rarely saw happen.

Jeff was understandably upset considering how long we had been looking for a house. But I actually started to laugh. I finally started to understand. I said, "This isn't our house. Something better is coming." I knew in my heart this was true. This is where we start to "know" and "trust" instead of "hope".

A week later another house came up for sale farther down the same street with more trees, more space, and bigger backyard. It was an old house but in good condition. It had all the things I wanted and the energy when we walked in was perfect. I knew in my heart this was our house. As we walked to the second floor I started to look around, and I opened a door I thought was a broom closet. Instead, it was a set of stairs leading up. My heart skipped a beat as I held my breath going up the stairs.

I saw the first window the same as I saw in my meditation. When I reached the top of the stairs, I turned around to find the matching window. The emotions I felt in that moment were overwhelming. It was confirmation that this was indeed our house. The attic wasn't finished the way I saw it in my mind, but I knew it was what we could do in the future.

It was a stressful evening as we were in a bidding war against someone who was offering more money. Ironically, we didn't end up being the highest bid but we still won. When we surrendered to the process and stopped trying to orchestrate, we manifested exactly where we were meant to be. We love it here and after we bought it, we found out we had friends all around us.

I wonder sometimes how much faster we would have been able to manifest our home if we fully surrendered to the universe. To trust that what was laid out for us was meant to be. If we had been more flexible instead of trying to orchestrate. I know it would have accelerated our progress exponentially. Collapsing time frames but I believe everything is timing. It was a valuable lesson that I now share with others so they can learn from my experience.

We all have experiences where we can help others learn from those mistakes so they can avoid them. Some experiences are unavoidable because this is how we grow. This is how we start to crawl, walk, and run. It is through the hardships we have experienced along the way. It is from experiencing life and learning from our mistakes. Reflecting on these pieces of wisdom life gives us. Not being angry by the experience and victimized from it but to be empowered by them. Some experiences are easier than others to see the wisdom upon reflection, but it is ours to harness.

Intentional Action

As we start moving forward with our plan we don't want to try to do everything all at once. One of the hardest things is to be selective in our actions. We tend to want to be overzealous in our efforts. This is great if there are a lot of things you want to do. Just don't try to do it all at once. It becomes a recipe for exhaustion and burnout.

The last thing I want you to do is to give up because you feel like there is lack of movement. This is where we want to be "intentional" with our actions, which will allow us to create stepping stones for lasting change in our life. It will help us to start walking toward our goals with intention. You want to focus on impact over fluff. I did the opposite, and it took time away from what mattered.

I need a website, I need a blog, I need this and that. Focusing all of my time on the things I thought were important but in the grand scheme of things they were not. We try to do a million different things. We think the more we do the more we will accomplish. Therefore, the more successful we will be. Yet when we try to do everything, it doesn't feel productive. It can also be discouraging to cross things off our list, but they are not moving the needle. When we come up against resistance, we tend to try to push harder. We think, "If I do more, create more, attend more events, this will make me successful."

Start to be aware of certain assumptions you might be making as you start walking toward your goals. Are these assumptions true or have they been put on me? When we start to shift our perspective around what we think is true, it can help us create a new reality. For example, many people equate success with grinding. We always have to do more. I counter this assumption. I have found doing less but focusing on the impact creates sustainable momentum.

This is what I teach my clients moving in alignment. When we come up against blocks or resistance, we don't force them. Instead, we unravel the blocks, shifting and transmuting them. Aligning and identifying new opportunities. I guide my clients to learn how to focus on the long-term impact. Why are you doing this? What is the ripple effect you want to create?

If one thing was going to move the needle, what would that be? If I want to incorporate my purpose within my life, where would I get the most joy? Incorporating purpose in our life creates more happiness, meaning, and enrichment in our lives. This is where we need to start.

If you begin a new career or role incorporating your purpose, what would that look like? What would bring you the most joy instead of work? I think most of us already create a lot of work projects in our life that are not benefiting us. But we continue to do them because that's how we've always done it. How can this be shifted to be fun? How can your intentional action create more meaning?

Start to think about how you can make the most impact. What is the path of least resistance? It sounds crazy but the simplest way forward is usually where you gain the most impact. As humans, we tend to want to overcomplicate things. We think if we do more complicated things, we will be more successful. Simplicity is the path of least resistance. Think of small and sustainable steps to get to your goal. This is where you are going to have help along the way. You have your support system. Don't try to do it alone.

I have done that path too, not wanting to bother people. Instead, I want you to start reaching out to the people in your life. The words we create are magical. They really do create opportunities. You don't know who can help you unless you ask. The worst thing that can happen is they say no. That's okay, because the best-case scenario is that they have a great opportunity waiting for you. They can put you in touch with someone who can open a door for you. This is the intentional action. Create space for support in your life and create opportunities to see where they lead.

When we start to live our life in a new direction, it can feel awkward or scary because we haven't done it before. We are not sure if it will work out. We are pushing outside our comfort zone. Focus on your own path and try not to get caught up in everyone else's journey. I found myself getting tripped up by what everyone else was doing and thinking I needed to replicate it. This was not a smart move. Instead of helping me, I went in so many different directions. I started to burn out while at the same time doubting myself.

Put up blinders or reminders to not get sucked down the path of others. It can be so easy to start looking at other people's lives and feel like you are lacking. You start to think, "I'm not where they are" or "They are so much further along than me." The truth is you will never be where they are because you are on your own trail. This path is unique to you.

You may question your direction, and this is where I will urge you to start checking in with yourself. We talked about using your intuition to find your purpose. You can apply this intuition before you make your decisions. Do a "gut check" to see if it aligns with you. Sometimes we are so quick to implement strategies because we see others doing it. Fear creeps into our mind making us feel inadequate that they know something we don't. Check in with your intuition because it doesn't come from a place of fear.

Following our intuition can be difficult because most of us were not taught to fully embrace it. We have relied a lot on our minds. Making logical choices and rolling the dice. Intuition may seem counter-logical. You may think that something didn't work out and therefore, your intuition isn't working. We still must experience challenges and hardships to grow and learn. Using our intuition isn't about us always taking the easiest path to our goals. It is about trusting the process and following the breadcrumbs. What I have found is the more we embrace our intuition, the stronger it becomes.

When we become in tune with our bodies, we can use it as a compass to guide us. Our intuition can lead us to solutions our mind cannot see. It can help us to shift our perspective and follow a different route. Our path to a new direction that is meant for us. Embrace this side of you and let go of what everyone else is doing. Sometimes we don't want to break from the flock because of fear. It is a herd mentality where we can be influenced to do what others are doing. Instead start moving forward in your own authentic truth.

Comparison can also make us doubt if we are on the right path. This can be especially true when you are on social media, particularly when you can get caught up in scrolling. You start overanalyzing everything and end up doing nothing. Limit how much time you spend on social media because it can be easy to get sucked in. I try to limit my social media intake to less than thirty minutes a day. Too much time on social media can make you feel unmotivated or that you are always behind the eight ball. You may think, "What if it is the wrong choice?" Remember, you can adjust, but you don't know until you start. This is how you learn and grow.

You got this! You are a unique individual who has so much to give to the world. Allow that light to shine through you in a unique way. Don't get stuck in the weeds trying to emulate everyone else. When we try to fit in a box that was never meant for us, it comes off as inauthentic.

That is the amazing thing about the world we live in. I can shine my light differently from yours and we can both succeed. What is the vision you want to hold? Focus on the impact you can make. When you start there and keep mindful of the joy you can create in your life, you will flourish.

Sacred "Yes"

The sacred yes is a simple technique but has a profound effect. The energy that resides within us vibrates at different frequencies. When our vibrations are higher from emotions like love and joy, it can create openings and opportunities through the energy we carry inside. However, when we are cutting ourselves off or blocking through our internal dialogue, this narrows our vision.

When we unconsciously put ourselves down, it creates a ripple effect. We rarely pay attention to the terrible and mean things we say to ourselves. It can create self-doubt, lowering our vibrations and creating states of doubting our choices. We miss opportunities because our focus resonates with fear. We are not in an expansive state so we can't see the hidden opportunities.

We can get stuck in our monotonous mind trying to keep us safe and protect us from the unknown. It can be a struggle unless we start to give ourselves permission to be in an expansive state. When you do this exercise, you will start to feel in the body the difference from when you are saying "no" to yourself and when you are giving a sacred "yes".

This is the state we need to be in to create higher frequencies, giving us new opportunities. When we are aware of the cycles of self-doubt holding us back, we can rephrase with "yes" at the end. It will give you a boost of energy to shift your mindset.

It can start to shift our energy from doubt to confidence. It is not something that is mastered overnight, but is a mastery through consistency. When we create consistent habits, we can start to create major shifts in our life. Using the sacred "yes" at the end of our sentences help us receive new opportunities.

For example, if someone is taking away your power, you can feel your energy being drained. You can create an affirmation, "I am taking back my power, YES!" The phrase is empowering and simple. Those who feel inadequate will try to explain away their confidence. They don't feel confident, so they overexplain. Our boundaries need no explanation.

This is when we start to change the trajectory of our life. When we are not trying to convince anyone of what we are doing. Instead, we believe in what we are doing. You can hear it with the conviction of our words. I am a coach, I am a business owner, I run a business, and I help people shine their light and lead from a place of wholeness. That's it, period.

I would say, "Well I lost my job, and I am trying to run a business, and I have gotten into coaching." When you are trying to explain away an answer, ask yourself who are you trying to convince? Because usually it is not the person you are talking to. Instead, we are trying to convince ourselves when we don't believe in what we are saying. This is when we need to create a sacred yes. This will open the channels to new opportunities that give us confidence. Even if we don't feel it in the moment.

Our mind tries to create a disconnect within ourselves; it will tell you all the reasons why you shouldn't pursue your dreams. Essentially, our mind tries to keep us safe by creating guard rails. While this can be helpful for us to logically understand our actions, these guardrails can quickly turn into prison bars.

Think of it as a river flowing toward your goals. Your actions and energy move you toward it. However, if we are constantly in a negative mindset, it slows down the flow of manifestation. This hidden element can greatly influence the speed with which we can create action and impact. Remember, doing more doesn't mean we will get the results faster.

This is why words create magic. They have a frequency that accelerates our progress or holds us back. It is a language we use, but it is the intention behind it that helps support our goals. Use your purpose and think about how you want to incorporate it within your life. Ask yourself, how can you start to incorporate your sacred yes to manifest what you want? How can your words support your ambitions and goals? How can you start to make this a reality? Start to say "YES" to yourself!

Consistency

One of the key aspects I have learned from taking intentional action is consistency. It can be easy to start and stop, but when we are in constant flow, it creates momentum, building micro habits that can support our growth and path. Experiment and see what works for you. Give yourself enough time to ensure what you are working on actually takes flight. You need time to start seeing results as your guiding force. If you try something once and it doesn't work out, it doesn't mean it is the wrong way forward, but it may need alterations.

You can learn a lot about yourself through this process, but action is a key step. If you don't take action because you are comparing yourself to everyone else, you will stand still. Take the first step, even if it doesn't go as planned. When we move forward, tweaking, learning, and experimenting, we can start building momentum. Remember, things can take time to build momentum, so don't give up.

In a society where we are trying to be perfect this can go against you. I spent so much time waiting and planning but what I really needed was to consistently put myself out there. Whether that is broadening your network and meeting new people. When we are consistent in our actions we can create more momentum. This can also help with our motivation because consistency builds habits.

It also allows you to start building resilience within yourself. As a Druid, one of the fundamental teachings is to never give up. Take a break for as long as you like, pivot, adapt, but continue to move forward. Especially when it involves living your purpose in whatever capacity works for you.

When I say never give up, it doesn't mean you should continue things that drain you or are not working. Instead, find new ways forward. We can shift how we are creating meaning in our life. How you want to live your life should be sustaining you and not draining you. This is how we can build those habits to support us through not only the good times but the hard times.

Consistency is a powerful tool, but that doesn't mean it's easy. It can be difficult to create sustainable habits. I developed the AIDE framework below to help you be more consistent. This will help you incorporate habits to live your purpose. It will help you overcome the procrastination and self-doubt that comes up. It will help you build momentum by consistently unravelling and shifting habits that are holding you back.

The AIDE Framework

1. Acknowledge

We first need to acknowledge where you are at. Everything starts with awareness. It allows us to know where we are going and to move forward. It is usually our own inability that prevents us from seeing where we currently are. We may not want to or feel embarrassed, judging ourselves for not being further along. This is a practice where you want to compassionately acknowledge. This takes out the judgement and allows you to be neutral. When we judge ourselves, it creates shame, resentment, and judgement that will only block your growth. Consider the following questions to gain clarity:

- Where is there a disconnect when you are trying to create momentum?
- Do you have certain habits supporting procrastination?
- Are these procrastinating habits triggered by a deeper root cause?
- What have you noticed are your main distractors?

- When things don't go your way, what is your initial reaction?

  o Do you want to give up?
  o Do you blame yourself?
  o Do you see it as a learning opportunity?

- What supports your motivation?

  o When do you feel energized?
  o What habits energize you?
  o Are there certain times of day you feel more motivated?

Start to build awareness around your thoughts. Take a day to set a timer hourly throughout the day and check in with yourself. What were you thinking about when the timer went off?

Once you have evaluated everything, make two lists. The first is your Spark list. These are the habits supporting you. They make you feel energized and help you to be in the moment. Next create your Draining list. They are habits that are not supporting you. They are dragging on your motivation and energy. They are blocking you.

2. Ignite the Sparks

Take a look at your Spark list. These are going to be your supporting habits. We are going to start leveraging them. For example, when I get stressed, one of my sparks is exercise, especially running. It helps to release excess energy that I may be carrying. It helps me focus and is active mediation for me.

I find when we don't feel like doing something to the best of our abilities, we don't do it at all. Give yourself permission to do a half-assed version. I know that sounds terrible for the perfectionists out there. If consistency is the goal, you are still going to build momentum even if you do a smaller version of one of your sparks. For example, if I didn't have the energy to do a full run, maybe I'll go for a walk around the block. It is better to stay consistent even if it is not to the full level you want. This starts to rewire your habits.

3. Discard bad habits

You want to start minimizing habits enabling procrastination and bringing down your motivation. I love it when I read self-help books, and their suggestion is to just stop bad habits. Why didn't I think of that? Anyone who has bad habits knows they are incredibly hard to break for a reason. Below are techniques that have helped me and my clients to weed out bad habits. Remember, this is an ongoing process. You are more likely to shed bad habits in layers instead of all at once. Some people can quit bad habits all at once and others have to work up to it, slowly transitioning them out of their life.

One of the first steps is identifying the habit you want to change. Choose one after doing the evaluation. Don't try to do them all at once because you will burn out. It will be like your New Year's resolutions all over again. Take baby steps. Habits are hard to break so be kind to yourself through this process.

Find the triggers

Find the triggers of your bad habit. For example, I had this bad habit of watching TV while eating. I hated this habit for so many reasons. Food is meant to be tasted and enjoyed in the present moment. So instead of breaking the habit directly, I focused on breaking the trigger. I tried very hard to eat in different rooms, like having dinner at the dining room table.

I would also create new triggers for the family room. Instead of watching television, I would use music as a positive trigger to paint instead. You want to start creating new triggers to be supportive. Again, each person is different so experiment with this technique.

Positive and negative impact

I would remind myself of the benefits of why this is helping me in the long run. What will you gain by giving up this bad habit? Is it more time to do something you love? Is it saving money you could put to better use? Are you strengthening your relationships by discontinuing this habit?

I would also remind myself what I am sacrificing by continuing this habit. How is it blocking you from achieving your goal? It can help us break bad habits when we can see how they negatively impact us. From a psychological standpoint, we hate to lose more than we gain. This perspective can help us to see how these habits are negatively affecting us.

What are you giving up by not evolving this habit and allowing more positive ones to support and take its place? For example, how much money are you spending on expensive habits like drinking, smoking, gambling, and THC? What is the dollar amount you are giving up on a yearly basis to continue these habits? What could that money go toward instead? A trip you always wanted to go on? Money toward a downpayment on a house?

When I added up all the movies or shows I watched in a year, I was astounded at the hours lost. One hour a day is 365 hours a year. This doesn't include those ten-part Netflix series you can binge watch in a day. It adds up and you barely realize how much time you are giving up. I would think about this each time I started to turn on the TV. In that amount of time, I could have learned a new language. Well, maybe not me because I am terrible at languages. But other people could learn a language. Shifting our perspective on what we are giving up can help us put in perspective what we are missing out on.

Create parameters

I also would limit my time on social media. If I wanted to engage in social media, I would set a timer on my phone restricting access to certain apps. The distractions and comparisons are endless unless we use tools to set boundaries. I use the app timers to close apps and refocus my energy.

Unravel the resistance

We tend to create bad habits in our life because there is something we don't want to see beneath the surface. When we are stressed, we may reach for a glass of wine to release tension instead of sitting with the feeling. When we are emotionally triggered, we use substances to numb the emotion that is coming up. Going deeper into the emotion can be uncomfortable.

When I worked for someone else, I never had an issue with procrastination. I was accountable to someone else. When I started to work for myself, I was the worst procrastinator because deep down I didn't think I was good enough. I would watch television or scroll through social media comparing myself to everyone because I didn't believe in myself. A lot of the time we use bad habits as a distraction because there is something we don't want to see. Usually, our inner critic.

Down the road

It can be easy to put off shifting our habits and creating consistency in our life that supports us. I can't tell you how many times I would say to myself, "Tomorrow. I can do it tomorrow. One more day won't make a difference." Trust me, this thought process will not serve you. Instead, I started to visualize the future and ask myself, "Do I still want to be here battling this same habit in a year?" My answer was always, "Fuck, no!" Seeing this habit in the future can also give us motivation to do something about it in the moment. This is where you make that small shift. Each shift creates a new version. Take it slow and keep going.

4. Execute - Just do it!

The fourth part of the process is to execute, just start doing it! It doesn't matter how small you start. Sometimes we try to start with too much. Focus on only executing a fraction. Sometimes we just need to start somewhere and build on our consistency. Perfection be damned and keep going. This helps us to build discipline. If we are consistent in our practices, they become habits and will get easier.

This is a skill cultivated by desire and experimentation. Find what works for you and adapt. Most importantly, don't give up. Consistency cultivates discipline. During the evaluation period be kind and compassionate to yourself. I went through phases where I would put myself down because I couldn't create consistency for myself.

It takes time and practice. It can feel disheartening at the beginning because you feel like you are not making progress. Remember that we are always moving forward. Energetically this creates momentum even if it feels like we are not where we want to be. Everything follows energy and manifests physically. Our thoughts are important to be aware of; keep this in mind as we start to move forward.

Consistency in gratitude also has a positive spiral effect. I know we hear a lot about gratitude, but it does create more abundance when we are able to be in higher vibrations. Sometimes it can be hard to see gratitude when we are in certain circumstances. When we have had a tough go of it or life throws us unimaginable curve balls. Consistency in these higher vibrations can help your momentum. It allows us to remember we are the ones who give ourselves permission to be happy now.

We tend to focus instead on the proverbial "when" to give us permission. When we put limitations on our happiness, we are waiting for something external to happen. When I have a certain job or title, a certain amount of money, a partner, a child, etc., then I will be happy. These external factors create a disconnect within us because we are never enough as is. It is the love we carry that dictates our happiness. Only we can consistently show up for ourselves to be our own love, our own happiness, and the gratitude of that love.

Ask if you have been denying yourself your own happiness. Denying yourself the ability to love yourself unconditionally. It takes a lot for us to look in the mirror and love ourselves exactly as we are. With all the flaws, all the cracks, or the parts we think are broken. Consistently grateful to be exactly as we are is no easy feat but the rewards of doing so can create wholeness.

There are multiple ways to be consistent that will help us in our pursuit of living our purpose. We can create momentum but continuously be intentional with our actions. We can create a practice of gratitude and self-love as we move through new challenges and changes within our life. We understand how the words we use create magic. Ensure you are saying "yes" to yourself, following your intuition, and allowing these opportunities to emerge.

Exercise: Intentional Action

How can you start to take more intentional action toward your goals? Answer the following questions and start to make a plan to implement them.

1. What steps can you take to live your purpose?
2. Based on the vision you created in the previous chapter, how can you create more impact with your actions?
3. How can you incorporate your "Sacred Yes" into each purposeful step?
4. How can you leverage the AIDE framework to help with consistency and build supportive habits in your life to build momentum?

Survey:

1. On a scale from 1-10 how are you currently feeling about your purpose?
2. On a scale from 1-10 Did you find clarity on your purpose?
3. On a scale from 1-10 How confident are you in taking the next step?

What's Next...

While we have come to the end of the book, this is not the end of your journey. This is just the beginning. You are now starting to walk your path to include your purpose. Feel proud of all the work you have accomplished by completing the exercises at the end of each chapter. You are well on your way to accomplishing your goals and creating a life of meaning.

Keep shining your light, my beautiful friend!

~Megs

www.fearlesslotus.com

The Next Step

If you haven't done so yet, I encourage you to take advantage of the bonus gift I mentioned at the beginning of this book.

To thank you for purchasing my book, I'm offering the *Find Your Purpose Workbook* along with guided meditations to support you on your journey. This interactive PDF is designed to help you get the most out of this book.

It will guide you as you work through the exercises at the end of each chapter. These practices are truly transformational, especially when we commit to putting the lessons into action.

To get exclusive access to these bonus materials, visit: **www.fearlesslotus.com/freegift**

References

AR, Sutin, Aschwanden D., Luchetti M., Stephan Y. and Terracciano. "Sense of Purpose in Life is Associated with Lower Risk of Incident Dementia." *Journal of Alzheimer's Disease* 83 no.1 (2021): 249–258. https://pmc.ncbi.nlm.nih.gov/articles/-PMC8887819.

Benefits Canada. "71% of Canadian Employees Considering Leaving Their Jobs in 2024: Survey." Last modified March 25, 2024, 09:00. www.benefitscanada.com/news/bencan/71-of-canadian-employees-considering-leaving-their-jobs-in-2024-survey.

Boreham, Ian D. and Nicola S. Schutte. "The Relationship Between Purpose in Life and Depression and Anxiety." Journal of Clinical Psychology 79 no. 12 (2023): 2736-2767. https://onlinelibrary.wiley.com/doi/full/-10.1002/jclp.23576.

Cable, Dan. "What You Should Follow Instead of Your Passion." *Harvard Business Review*. November 24, 2020. https://hbr.org/2020/11/what-you-should-follow-instead-of-your-passion.

Cable, Daniel M., Francesca Gino and Bradley R. Staats. "Breaking Them in or Eliciting Their Best? Reframing Socialization around Newcomers' Authentic Self-expression." *Administrative Science Quarterly* 58 no.1 (2013) 1-36. https://doi.org/10.1177/0001839213477098.

Charles-Leija, Humberto, Carlos G. Castro, Mario Toledo, and Rosalinda Ballesteros-Valdés. "Meaningful Work, Happiness at Work, and Turnover Intentions." *International Journal of Environmental Research and Public Health* 20 no. 4 (2023):17-20. https://pmc.ncbi.nlm.nih.gov/articles/PMC9963286.

Diehl, Manfred, Elizabeth L. Hay, and Kathleen M. Berg. "The Ratio between Positive and Negative Affect and Flourishing Mental Health across Adulthood." *Aging Ment Health* 15 No. 7 (2011): 882-893. www.tandfonline.com/doi-/abs/10.1080/13607863.2011.569488.

Goleman, Daniel. "Therapists Find Many Achievers Feel They're Fakes." *The New York Times*. Sept. 11, 1984. https://www.nytimes.com/1984/09/11/science/therapists-find-many-achievers-feel-they-re-fakes.html.

Gollwitzer, Peter M. and Veronika Brandstatter. "Implementation Intentions and Effective Goal Pursuit." *Journal of Personality and Social Psychology* 73 no.1 (1997): 186-199. https://sparq.stanford.edu/sites/g/files/sbiybj19021/files/media/file/gollwitzer_brandstatter_1997_-_implementation_intentions_effective_goal_pursuit.pdf.

Harvard Health Publishing. "Giving Thanks Can Make You Happier." *Harvard Medical School*, August 14, 2021. https://www.health.harvard.edu/healthbeat/giving-thanks-can-make-you-happier.

Hill, Patrick L., Nicholas A. Turiano, Daniel K. Mroczek, and Anthony L. Burrow. "The Value of a Purposeful Life: Sense of Purpose Predicts Greater Income and Net Worth." *Journal of Research in Personality* 65 (2016): 38-42. https://doi.org/10.10-16/j.jrp.2016.07.003.

Holt-Lunstad, Julianne, Theodore Robles, David A Sbarra. "Advancing Social Connection as a Public Health Priority in the United States." *American Psychologist* 72 no. 6 (2017): 517–530. https://psycnet.apa.org/-doiLanding?-doi=10.1037%2Famp0000103.

Holt-Lunstad, Julianne, Timothy B. Smith, Mark Baker, Tyler Harris, David Stephenson. "Loneliness and Social Isolation as Risk Factors for Mortality: a Meta-Analytic Review." *Perspectives on Psychological Science* 10 no. 2 (2015): 227-237. https://journals.sagepub.com/doi/10.1177/1745691614568352.

Jang, Jihoon, Seong Yong Park, Yeon Yong Kim, Eun Ji Kim, Gusang Lee, Jihye Seo, Eun Jin Na Jae-Young Park, Hong Jin Jeon. "Risks of suicide among family members of suicide victims: A nationwide sample of South Korea." *Front. Psychiatry* 13 (2022): https://doi.org/10.3389/fpsyt.2022.995834.

Kahneman, Daniel and Angus Deaton. "High Income Improves Evaluation of Life but Not Emotional Well-being." *PNAS Early Edition*, Princeton University (2010): 3-5. https://www.princeton.edu/~deaton-/downloads/deaton_kahneman_high-_income_improves_evaluation_August2010.pdf.

Kim, Eric S., Ying Chen, Julia S. Nakamura, Carol D. Ryff, and Tyler J. VanderWeele. "Sense of Purpose in Life and Subsequent Physical, Behavioral, and Psychosocial Health: An Outcome-Wide Approach." *American Journal of Health Promotion* 36 no. 1 (2021): 137–147. https://-pmc.ncbi-.nlm.-nih.gov/articles/PMC8669210.

McDonnell, Sharon, Sandra Flynn, Jenny Shaw, Shirley Smith, Barry McGale, Isabelle M. Hunt. "Suicide bereavement in the UK: Descriptive findings from a national survey." *Suicide Life Threat Behav* 52 no. 5 (2022):887-897. https://online-library.wiley.com/doi/10.1111/sltb.12874.

Murthy, Vivek "Our Epidemic of Loneliness and Isolation." *U.S. Department of Health and Human Services* (2023): 1-81. https://www.hhs.gov/sites/default/files/surgeon-general-social-connection-advisory.pdf.

Statistics Canada. "How happy are Canadians?" Last modified March 20, 2024, 2:00 p.m. (EDT). https://www.statcan-gc.ca/o1/en/plus/5891-how-happy-are-canadians.

Van den Broeck, Anja, Willy Lens, Hans De Witte, Hermina Van Coillie. "Unraveling the Importance of the Quantity and the Quality of Workers' Motivation for Well-Being: A Person-Centered Perspective." Journal of Vocational Behavior 82 (2013): 69-78. https://selfdetermination theory.org/SDT/documents/2013_VandenBroeckLensetal _JOVB.pdf.

Thank You

Before you go, I want to say thank you for purchasing my book and spending your valuable time with me. I know there are countless books to choose from and limited hours in the day, so I'm deeply grateful you chose to journey through mine. I hope it was beneficial, enlightening, and offered you new insights about yourself.

If you enjoyed what you've read, I would be so grateful for your support. Please take a moment to leave a review on Amazon. It would be greatly appreciated.

Your feedback means so much to me. It helps me grow as a writer and gives me the chance to create more books that speak to your journey. Most of all, it supports you as you continue to transform and walk your unique path.

With heartfelt gratitude,

~ Megs

About the Author

Meghan Walsh is an empowered leadership coach, keynote speaker, and educator with over 18 years of experience in marketing, communications, and leadership development. She built a marketing department from scratch for a Fortune 500 company. She has led high-performing teams across diverse industries, driving business growth through data-driven strategies and meaningful engagement.

Beyond the corporate world, Meghan is dedicated to personal transformation and empowerment. As a certified Positive Psychology Practitioner, she also draws from her studies in Druidism, shamanism, and energy healing to help leaders cultivate confidence, authenticity, and purpose. By blending strategic insight with intuitive guidance, she supports professionals in leadership growth, career transitions, and personal development.

Connect with her at:

www.fearlesslotus.com

www.linkedin.com/in/megswalsh

www.instagram.com/fearless.lotus

Interested in one-to-one coaching to elevate your leadership and step into the purpose-driven career you've been longing for?

Email her at **fearlesslotusgroup@gmail.com**

Client Recommendations

"Meghan is truly a gem! Her style of coaching and empowerment is so natural and easy, she is definitely doing what she was meant to do in this world! I hired her for career and professional coaching, and I have experienced such a profound difference in the way I approach my sales, my work and my purpose. In such a short amount of time, we've uncovered so many things that were blocking me from reaching my full potential.

The most beautiful breakthrough I experienced with her was unlocking my intuition and utilizing it for business - that was totally not in my cards but now that it's here, I am excited to keep developing it. Meghan is kind, compassionate, powerful and very intuitive. Truly a gem, and anyone who works with her will get this right from the start!"

~ Kristine Ajami

"Meghan led a truly inspiring and impactful session for our group that left me feeling both energized and deeply grounded—a rare and powerful combination! Working with her in the lead-up to the event was equally rewarding. Meghan is gracious, joyful, and incredibly generous with her time and insights. I wholeheartedly recommend partnering with Meghan, whether personally or professionally—she brings a unique blend of warmth, wisdom, and presence to everything she does."

~ Autumn Kerr

"I had the pleasure of working with Meghan for our first learning week. Meghan was a great partner and support. She led two sessions, one on imposter syndrome, and one focused on shifting mindset. She brought fresh insights and created a real connection with our audience through content that was both engaging and actionable. I would highly recommend her as a speaker and facilitator. She brings insight, professionalism, and true partnership."

~ Michelle Tucker

www.ingramcontent.com/pod-product-compliance
Lightning Source LLC
Chambersburg PA
CBHW071154160426
43196CB00011B/2079